The Politics and Strategy of the Second World War

A series edited by
Noble Frankland and Christopher Dowling

GREECE
1940-1941

Charles Cruickshank, MA, DPhil, FRHistS,
was born in Fyvie in 1914 and educated at
Aberdeen University, Hertford College,
Oxford, and Edinburgh University. His
subsequent distinguished career in the Civil
Service has been equalled by his success
both as a writer and a historian. A contributor
to a number of historical periodicals, he is
also the author of *Elizabeth's Army* (1946,
1966), the standard work on the sixteenth-
century English army; *Army Royal: Henry
VIII's Invasion of France 1513* (1969); *The
English Occupation of Tournai 1513-1519* (1971);
and a co-author of *A Guide to the Sources of
British Military History* (1971). Tending towards
more recent history, Dr Cruickshank is the
author of *The German Occupation of the
Channel Islands* (Official History), published
in 1975 on the thirtieth anniversary of the
liberation of those islands.

CHARLES CRUICKSHANK

GREECE
1940-1941

NEWARK
University of Delaware Press

FIRST AMERICAN EDITION PUBLISHED 1979

Associated University Presses, Inc.
Cranbury, New Jersey 08512

Library of Congress Catalogue Card Number: 79-52239
ISBN 0-87413-159-6

PRINTED IN THE UNITED STATES OF AMERICA

CONTENTS

MAPS

EDITORS' INTRODUCTION

Numerous books and articles have been written about the weapons, battles and campaigns of the Second World War, and the problems of command, supply and intelligence have been extensively surveyed. Yet, though the fighting has been so fully described from these and other points of view, the reasons why the various military operations took place have attracted less study and remain comparatively obscure. It is to fill this gap in the understanding of the Second World War that this series has been conceived.

The perceptive have always understood the extent to which war is a continuation of policy by other means, and the clash of armies or fleets has, in intention, seldom been haphazard. Battles and campaigns often contain the keys to the understanding of the grand strategies of supreme commands and the political aims and purpose of nations and alliances.

In each of the volumes in this series an important battle or campaign is assessed from the point of view of discovering its relationship to the war as a whole, for in asking the questions Why was this battle fought? and What effect did it produce? one is raising the issue of the real meaning and character of the war.

As the series progresses, its readers, advancing case by case, will be able to make general judgements about the central character of the Second World War. Some will find this worthwhile in its own right; others will see it as a means of increasing their grasp of the contemporary scene. Thirty years have now passed since the death of Hitler and the capitulation of Japan. These momentous events were the culmination of a war which transformed

Greece *1940-1941*

the political and social, the economic and technological and, indeed, the general conditions of society and politics in virtually every corner of the world.

NOBLE FRANKLAND
CHRISTOPHER DOWLING

I

1. Objectives

Hitler's objectives in the Balkans were to neutralize, preferably by diplomacy, countries whose active support he could not enlist; to prevent a regional war which would absorb forces needed for his attack on Russia; to secure the supply of raw materials, especially oil from Romania, on which the Axis powers depended; to limit Russia's territorial gains in the Balkans; and to forestall any attempts by the British to establish themselves there.

After Italy's entry into the war in June 1940 his task was made the more delicate by Mussolini's anxiety to achieve a military success which would give him a more important voice at the peace conference – seemingly just round the corner. Age-old enmities which had many times plunged the Balkans into war had been imperfectly buried between the two world wars. It would take little to bring them to the surface again. The Duce's irresponsible aspirations might lead to a Balkan conflict that would endanger German long-term plans. He must therefore be carefully watched and kept in line.

Britain's objectives were to deny to the Axis powers the domination of the eastern Mediterranean which could win the war for them. This might be done by building a common front in the Balkans against Germany and Italy, again preferably by diplomacy. But it was not a straight diplomatic contest. The Germans had the well-trained, well-equipped, all-conquering Wehrmacht behind them. The British were struggling for existence with unseasoned troops. Diplomacy is more likely to succeed when a powerful and ruthless army stands in the wings. Hitler was playing from a hand of great strength. Churchill's could hardly have been weaker.

9

2. Balkan kaleidoscope

The Balkan countries to which the opposing great powers looked for support had been chopped and changed in the first quarter of the century. In 1913 the Ottoman Empire lost Macedonia to Greece, and Thrace to Bulgaria, leaving Turkey with only a small foothold in Europe. In 1922 Thrace passed to Greece. North of Macedonia there was set up in 1918 the Kingdom of the Croats, Slovenes and Serbs, which in 1929 became Yugoslavia. Hungary, in addition to losing to the new kingdom Slovenia and Croatia in the west, lost Transylvania in the east to Romania, which in 1920 gained Bessarabia from Russia.

The entities created by these changes were not based on homogeneous ethnic groupings – which was virtually impossible, given the mixture of races in the area. This, and the fact that there were large German minorities in some countries, made it difficult for the newly-shaped states to settle down to stable political life. No country was sure of itself, each suspected its neighbour, and after the outbreak of war in 1939 all looked to Germany with a greater or lesser degree of subserviency. Perhaps only Greece was an exception to the rule of fear.

Hungary, having lost most, had the strongest incentive for a new shake-up in the peninsula. Her Regent, Horthy, made overtures to Hitler in November 1939. He said that men of sound judgement had realized that if negotiation failed the injustices of the peace settlement after the first world war would have to be wiped out by force of arms. Negotiation *had* failed. The League of Nations had ignored Hungary's grievances. When the whole world turned against Germany after her collapse in 1919, Hungary remained her only true friend. Yet Germany's attitude towards Hungary had changed. There was, for example, a movement to stir up Hungarian citizens of German origin because of the false accusations that minorities were being oppressed. The Hungarians were grateful and absolutely reliable, well aware of their debt to Germany. Everything they could spare was at the Führer's disposal.

With this letter Horthy sent a gift of fruit which he hoped Hitler would not consider naïve in these dark days; and, perhaps to avoid the risk of liquidating the Führer before his world conquest was well under way, he took the precaution of adding a warning postscript. The grapes had been sprayed and must therefore be well washed before they were eaten.[1]

Romania found herself in trouble with Germany at the beginning of the war. She incurred Foreign Minister Ribbentrop's grave displeasure for not dealing strictly enough with refugees from conquered Poland, and in particular for allowing President Moscicki to go to Switzerland. Further, Hitler regarded King Carol as an unreliable man with whom he could establish no personal relationship. The countries, however, were important to each other, and the difficulty over the refugees was forgotten. Germany needed oil and grain from Romania; and Romania needed armaments which Germany could now readily supply from booty won in Poland. Romania also looked to Germany for protection against Russia. Here again the countries were at one, since it was vital for Germany to see peace maintained within Romania. A Russian attack to recover Bessarabia would lead to the destruction of the oilfields, for the Romanian government had decided that in the event of invasion all production facilities would be demolished. This would be a major disaster for Germany.

The Bulgarians informed the Germans on 18 September 1939 that they would remain benevolently neutral. At the same time their Chargé d'Affaires in Berlin (Karastoyanov) asked Woermann, the Director of the Political Department of the Foreign Ministry, what Bulgaria should do if Russia took back Bessarabia, a move which he assumed the Romanians, profiting from the example of Poland, would not resist; and if they offered to Bulgaria Dobruja, the territory bordering the Black Sea immedi-

[1] *Documents on German Foreign Policy (Series D)* vol. viii, pp. 376-8.

ately south of the Danube. Woermann temporized. He said he saw no sign of an imminent occupation of Bessarabia by the Russians; but if it looked like happening Bulgaria should at once confer with Germany. Shortly after this Russia offered Bulgaria a mutual assistance pact. King Boris rejected the offer and asked Germany what line he should take if it were renewed. He was told that the German government could not answer a hypothetical question. They expected, however, that Bulgaria would conduct her affairs so that she did not come into conflict with the Soviet Union. If she did fall foul of the Russians, she could not look to Germany for support, in spite of their friendship.[2]

Although Prince Paul, who had been Regent since 1934, was a very weak character, and although Yugoslavia had economic importance for Germany, she was not yet caught in Hitler's net. She was a house divided. The Serbs in her population were markedly anti-German, unlike the Croats; and it would have been difficult for even a strong government to carry the whole people one way or the other. In September 1939 Göring ordered a go-slow in the delivery of arms to Yugoslavia under an agreement made earlier in the year; but he later agreed to send substantial quantities in return for copper, lead, tin, zinc, and hemp. At the end of September Paul expressed satisfaction about the delivery of arms, and said that the exchange of goods between the two countries must be promoted in every way.

In January 1940 the Yugoslav Foreign Minister (Cincar-Markovic) assured the German Minister in Yugoslavia (Heeren) that his country's relations with Germany were happily settled on the basis of economic ties and good neighbourliness. In April the Prince Regent spoke to Heeren of his love for Germany, German culture, and the German people; and expressed admiration for Germany's recent military successes. Fair words were not enough, however, and two months later Heeren told the

[2] *DGFP* viii, pp. 93, 484-5, 533-4.

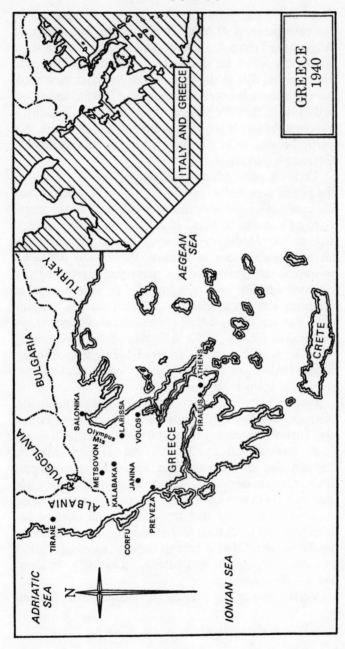

GREECE
1940

ITALY AND GREECE

ADRIATIC
SEA

N

IONIAN SEA

ALBANIA

YUGOSLAVIA

BULGARIA

TURKEY

AEGEAN
SEA

GREECE

CRETE

TIRANE

CORFU

PREVEZA

JANINA

KALABAKA

METSOVON

Olympus
Mts

SALONIKA

LARISSA

VOLOS

PIRAEUS

ATHENS

German Foreign Ministry that he was disappointed by the slow progress of Yugoslavia into the Axis camp. In August the Prince Regent was still singing the praises of the Reich, which he saw as being manifestly invincible. He accepted that in the long run Balkan countries would have to choose between Germany and Russia, and it was self-evident that Yugoslavia must opt for Germany – although the whole population did not yet agree with this, partly because of Francophile tendencies and mistrust of Germany's partner Italy.[3]

Turkey's geographical position put her at the end of the line of potential Axis victims or allies in south eastern Europe. She agreed with Britain and France in September 1939 to come to their aid if a European power brought war to the Mediterranean area. On 3 November the German Ambassador in Ankara (Papen) was instructed to inform the Turks that Germany was astonished that they were taking an Anglo-French line at a time when Germany was at war with Britain and France. Their conduct was a grave violation of the duties of a power not involved in the war, and a deliberate affront to Germany. The German government reserved the right to take any measures they saw fit if the treaties led to practical consequences against the Reich.

When the recently-appointed Turkish Ambassador (Gerede) called on Ribbentrop on 11 November to express the Turkish President's congratulations on Hitler's escape from assassination in Munich the Foreign Minister claimed that Turkey had now joined the anti-German front. Gerede denied it. The treaties with Britain and France were in no way directed against Germany. Ribbentrop went on to say that the assassination attempt had been inspired by Britain and added that the Ambassador would no doubt do his best to improve German-Turkish relations, although he had entered on his office at a very unfavourable time.

Turkey continued to steer an uneasy course between

[3] *DGFP* viii, 49-50, 163, 586-7; ix, 148; x, 546-7.

the Axis and the allies, while both sides worked hard to move her towards them. The Germans pointed out in March 1940 that her agreements with Britain and France might lead her to take up arms on their behalf if Italy came into the war; but the agreements provided that she was not obliged to help them if that seemed likely to involve her in armed conflict with the Soviet Union. Therefore Papen's line must be that Russia was waiting to pounce, and that if Turkey went to the aid of the allies it would be used by the Russians as an excuse to invade her.[4]

Germany continued to be heavily dependent on Turkish chromium; and in the middle of 1940 the two countries negotiated an economic agreement which was welcomed by the Turks, who needed all the trade they could get. The Germans assiduously used the economic weapon to try to detach Turkey from the allies, and made it clear that so long as the Turks placed their bets on England (Papen's phrase) there was no incentive to expand trade between Germany and Turkey.[5] It was hoped, however, that the new agreement would build a bridge to better political relations.

The protocol about the possibility of conflict with the Soviet Union in Turkey's agreements with Britain and France, which was supposed to be secret, was announced to the world by the Turks. This was playing the Germans' game since it was a clear indication to the Rusians that the Turks had an escape clause, and that they would almost certainly use it to preserve their neutrality to the last. In fact, after the fall of France the Turks argued that since she was no longer able to play her part in implementing the agreements, they were no longer operative, although it might have been argued that in the new circumstances they became in honour more binding than before.

The Turkish government did, however, declare that Turkey would remain non-belligerent, which was a good

[4] *DGFP* viii, pp. 371-2, 398-9; ix, 27-8.
[5] *Ibid.* x, p. 279.

deal better than nothing from Britain's point of view. Had the Turks thrown in their lot with Germany – chancing a violent reaction from Russia – and offered a free passage for an attack on Syria, it could have led to German control of the Suez Canal. The Turks took a bolder line when their own interests were directly at stake. If Italy attacked Greece they would observe friendly neutrality towards the latter; but a Bulgarian attack on Greece would immediately bring them into the war. Shortly afterwards, however, this was weakened into a statement that if Bulgaria declared war on Greece the position would have to be examined.

Greece was formally neutral, with a bias in favour of Britain. She was also, in Mussolini's eyes, too poor for the Italians to covet, at least in September 1939.[6] When Germany warned her in October 1939 that to charter her merchant fleet to Britain would be regarded as a serious departure from neutrality, Metaxas, the Minister President, replied that he could not stop private shipowners from chartering their ships where they chose. But Metaxas was concerned with the survival of Greece rather than with the survival of Britain. In February 1940 the Greek Minister in Germany (Rizo-Rangabé) was instructed to assure the German government that Greece would preserve her neutrality with all her strength to the very last; and to add that she hoped to expand her trade with Germany. In June of the same year Metaxas made a curious approach to the German Foreign Ministry through a German with business interests in Athens. The idea was that Germany should restrain Italy from attacking Greece, and guarantee Greek territory. The Foreign Ministry decided, however, that amateur politics were dangerous and refused to pursue the matter. If Greece wanted protection she must openly declare herself on the side of the Axis.[7]

[6] Ciano, *Diary*, p. 151.
[7] *DGFP* ix, pp. 514-16, 533.

3. Judgement of Solomons: the Vienna arbitration

Bessarabia was the first of the disputed territories to
change hands. In May 1940 King Carol, worried by troop
concentrations in Russia and Hungary near the borders of
Romania, tried to associate his country more closely with
Germany. Ribbentrop, however, quickly disposed of the
idea that he would be given armed help. If he wanted
peace he had better give way to Russia with a good grace.
On 27 June the Soviet Union formally made their long-
expected demand for the return of Bessarabia, and also
for northern Bukovina to which they had no real claim.
Ribbentrop instructed the German Minister in Bucharest
(Fabricius) to urge the Romanians to yield both territories
in order to avoid war with Russia.

When the instructions reached the German Legation
Fabricius was in audience with the King, who was complaining that Hitler had discouraged him from seeking a
rapprochement with Russia. He had therefore not sought
to clear up the question of Russia's claim to Bessarabia,
and considered that Germany was to blame for Romania's
predicament. Fabricius vigorously disclaimed all responsibility. When he asked what Carol would say to the
Russians the King answered that it would depend on the
extent of the help provided by Germany.

At this point Ribbentrop's message was delivered to
Fabricius, and read out by him. When he had finished

> The King was dismayed. He launched forth into critic-
> ism of our policy. How could we ask him to cede one-
> third of his territory without a fight? After all, he had
> obtained the Führer's word. The policy of the Reich was
> unreliable. I interrupted the King. As a representative
> of the Reich I could not listen to such rash words from
> His Majesty.

Later in the day the Minister President apologized to
Fabricius for the King's outburst – he had been deeply
affected by Germany's attitude, and had spoken in the

first heat of excitement. Romania would give way to the Russians demands.[8]

On 2 July Carol told Hitler that he had abandoned the guarantees given by Britain and France, and now wanted close collaboration with Germany in all fields. 'I take recourse to the assistance of the Führer and request him to help and protect us in these trying times'. No doubt the Romanians hoped that abject surrender might encourage Germany to defend them against the territorial claims of Hungary and Bulgaria; but they were to be disappointed. The Reich had succeeded in keeping war from Romania for the time being, and her oil would continue to flow uninterrupted; but it was now up to her to stand on her own feet and peacefully settle her differences with Hungary and Bulgaria. German policy was to let the Balkans stew in their own juice, so long as it did not boil over.[9]

This was risky, for a conflict that interrupted supplies of Romanian oil and grain was intolerable from the German point of view; but at first Hitler was content to leave the three disputants to come to a settlement among themselves. The dangers of this line soon became apparent. The Hungarian Minister in Germany (Sztojay) told the Foreign Ministry on 27 June that if the cession of Bessarabia to Russia was not matched by a parallel concession to Hungary it would lead to 'quite unforeseeable consequences'. Hungary wished, or rather *intended*, to ensure that Romania agreed to her just demands. On the same day the Bulgarian Minister (Draganov) mentioned Bulgaria's territorial ambitions. Both were told that the last thing Germany wanted was war in the Balkans. Draganov observed that his government would find themselves in a very difficult position if they were not allowed to strike while the iron was hot.[10]

On 1 July Ribbentrop told the German Minister in Hungary (Erdmannsdorf) that he assumed that Hungary would not run the risk of war for the sake of her revisionist

[8] *DGFP* x, pp. 36-7.
[9] *Ibid.* p. 91.
[10] *Ibid.* pp. 37-8.

demands. Therefore no positive action was called for. This was an error of judgement, for within twenty-four hours news of serious incidents along the Romanian-Hungarian border reached Berlin. Ribbentrop was forced to send new instructions. The Hungarians were to be told that while the Reich had no political interest in the Balkans the peninsula must not become a theatre of war. Germany had welcomed the peaceful agreement between Romania and the Soviet Union, and she sympathized with Hungary's revisionist demands; but in no circumstances was Romania to be attacked. If Hungary invaded her neighbour it would be entirely on her own responsibility. All this was couched in polite diplomatic language, but it added up to a powerful ultimatum. There was, however, some sugar on the pill. Ribbentrop said that he believed that revision would be possible at a more convenient time, and that Germany would then support Hungary's demands.[11]

Fabricius in Bucharest was instructed to find out if Romania was willing to negotiate with Hungary and Bulgaria; and to remind Carol that it was only thanks to a tragic disaster – the defeat of Germany in the first world war – that his territory had been extended at the expense of these countries. Further, Romania would never be strong enough to control areas with large Hungarian and Bulgarian minorities which wanted to be re-incorporated in their homelands. The King agreed that negotiations should begin at once, but still hoped that the Führer would discourage the other parties from carrying their demands beyond the bounds of justice and reason.[12]

During the next two months there was intensive diplomatic activity by the Germans to prevent Hungary and Bulgaria from going to war with Romania. Hitler and Ciano saw the Hungarian Minister President (Teleki) and Foreign Minister (Csaky) in Munich on 10 July. Hitler told them that there was nothing to stop Hungary from attacking Romania, provided that she was prepared to

[11] *DGFP* x, pp. 85-6.
[12] *Ibid.* pp. 116-17.

take the consequences; but it would be far better to negotiate. The Hungarians agreed to make sacrifices for the sake of maintaining peace in the Balkans, which they knew the Axis wanted. To help things along, Hitler wrote to Carol on 5 July recommending that he should seek 'a reconciliation in good faith with Hungary and Bulgaria'.[13]

On 26 July it was the turn of the Romanian Minister President to be lectured by Hitler and Ribbentrop. If a solution of the outstanding problems with Hungary and Bulgaria was not reached soon, the consequences might be serious. Next day they saw the Bulgarian Minister President (Filov) and told him that there had been some plain speaking with the Romanians, who might now be ready to come to terms with Bulgaria.[14]

Romania and Hungary, however, continued to jockey for position, each hoping for active German support. They began half-hearted negotiations with each other, but on 24 August the German Minister in Hungary reported to Berlin that they had been broken off and that if the Axis powers did not intervene Hungary and Romania would be at war within a week. Three days later the Hungarian Minister in Germany confirmed that a military solution was now contemplated. He asked, if it came to war, whose side would Germany take?

The question was academic, since in spite of Hitler's repeated assertions that he had no political interest in the Balkans, Germany could not allow it to come to war. Ribbentrop summoned the Hungarian Minister President and Foreign Minister to Vienna to tell them that the Axis powers were now prepared to arbitrate. Ciano was also present. Ribbentrop said that there was no doubt that if Hungary and Romania went to war the Russians would come in. Romania would be overrun and the Hungarian army would find itself face to face with Russian troops. He need not tell them what *that* would mean.

Hungary must remember that Germany was engaged in a life and death struggle with the British Empire which

[13] *DGFP* x, pp. 217-20.
[14] *Ibid.* pp. 307-16, 332-6.

took precedence over any squabbles in the Balkans. The Führer was about to attack England and expected that friendly nations would subordinate their own desires to this great objective, the attainment of which would benefit them all. In any case, whatever happened between Hungary and Romania Germany would see that she got all the Romanian oil she needed. Ribbentrop ended by saying that he and Ciano were busy men. Hungary must agree forthwith to accept arbitration, so that the award might be made the following day.

There followed an acrimonious discussion, the trend of which suggests that the Hungarian representatives feared that they were going to come off worst in the arbitration. Finally Ribbentrop said that if the parties refused arbitration, matters would have to take their course – which would be unpleasant for all concerned. There was no answer to this, and the Hungarians, having telephoned to their colleagues in Budapest, gave in. The Romanians had earlier agreed to arbitration, knowing equally that they dare not refuse. The award was made on 30 August and accepted by Csaky for Hungary and by Manoïlescu (their Foreign Minister) for Romania.[15]

Two-thirds of Transylvania went to Hungary. Romanian nationals living there automatically acquired Hungarian citizenship unless they opted for Romanian nationality within six months. Under a separate arrangement southern Dobruja was returned to Bulgaria. Although according to the communiqué arbitration had been carried out at the request of the Royal Romanian and Royal Hungarian governments the whole operation was more like knocking together the heads of two unruly schoolboys. However the affair was dressed up it had enabled Germany to prevent a Balkan war at the eleventh hour by buying off Hungary at the expense of Romania. In Britain the War Cabinet took the view that these changes in the map of the Balkans had been accomplished by aggression and compulsion, and could not be recogn-

[15] *DGFP* x, pp. 534-5, 553-5, 566-70.

ized. According to Ciano the Hungarians could not contain their joy when they saw the map defining the new frontiers. 'Then we heard a loud thud. It was Manoilescu, who fainted on the table. Doctors, massage, camphorated oil. Finally he comes to, but shows the shock very much'.[16]

The Regent of Hungary thanked the Führer for the results of the arbitration in suitably grovelling terms. 'The embattled Greater German Reich, animated by a feeling of true responsibility, has devoted its energies to a problem which does not directly affect its interests and has thus performed a duty for all of Europe.' An old wrong had been righted by a historic decision.[17] His letter was delivered to Hitler on 10 September by the Hungarian Minister, Sztojay. The Führer was delighted to take the credit and went on to review the current situation. If the Axis powers lost the war, which was of course impossible, the recent territorial adjustments would go by the board. Therefore Hungary must remain loyal to the Axis. There would have been no need to support Romania at all, had it not been for her oil. Germany could get by without it, but it was vital to Italy – Germany's ally for better or worse; and if it went up in flames it would be a psychological boost for Britain. For these reasons he and the Duce had decided themselves to protect the valuable oilfields and guarantee the new Romania.

Hitler had one piece of advice for Hungary. Her treatment of the German minority had not been too satisfactory. She must now treat her Volksdeutsch better. It would cost her nothing, and would considerably strengthen her position.[18]

One of the consequences of the rout of Romania was the abdication of King Carol and the succession to the throne of his son Mihai. The country was, however, effectively run by General Ion Antonescu, the Minister President, who was strongly pro-German. Fabricius considered that only Antonescu could save the country from chaos

[16] Ciano, p. 287.
[17] *DGFP* xi, pp. 7-8.
[18] *Ibid.* pp. 49-54.

and advised him to assume dictatorial powers and 'remove the universally-hated entourage of the King'. After prolonged discussions on 5 September Carol signed decrees which repealed the constitution of 1938 and left the monarchy with no more than ceremonial duties; and next day he abdicated.

To avoid a repetition of friction which might spark off war in the Balkans it was necessary to strengthen the German hold over the region. In September 1940 General von Tippelskirch of the German General Staff discussed with Antonescu, who was now firmly in the saddle as Leader of the State in Romania, the sending of a German military mission and troops. The proposal was accepted and Hitler agreed that army and Luftwaffe missions and a division should be sent. Their ostensible tasks would be to instruct the Romanian forces, but their real task, which was to be kept secret, was to protect the oilfields and to prepare for the deployment of German and Romanian troops in the event of war with Russia. German diplomatic missions were instructed to deny that this move was in any way anti-Soviet and to emphasize that it *was* anti-British.

The Italians, who first heard of the German move through broadcast news reports, took umbrage; and were little comforted by Ribbentrop's explanation that it had been necessary to keep the movement of troops secret lest it should encourage the British to bomb the Romanian oilfields.

4. Mussolini controlled

Hitler had made it abundantly clear by word and deed to every country in the Balkans that Germany *must* have peace in the region. Any government that ignored his wishes did so at their peril. It was not easy to keep in peaceful balance the component parts of the peninsula, with their complex multi-dimensional hatreds and aspirations; but in spite of the difficulties, aided by a team of highly-professional diplomats, he succeeded for over a year. At times he skated on very thin ice. Bessarabia was thrown to the Russians to keep them quiet. Romania was dismembered, and the pieces thrown to Hungary and Bulgaria to keep *them* quiet. Carol was frightened off the throne of Romania and replaced by a pro-Axis head of state. Economic links were forged with Yugoslavia, Turkey and Greece, partly because Germany needed their raw materials and partly to diminish any incentive they might have to join the allies. On the first anniversary of the outbreak of war it looked as if the Führer could launch Operation *Barbarossa* knowing that there would be no threat to the southern flank of his armies as they advanced into Russia.

He had not reckoned, however, with the irresponsible ambitions of his ally. From the beginning of the war Mussolini saw himself eventually playing the major role in the Mediterranean and the Balkans, to which the Führer could hardly object. On 23 September 1939 the Italian Ambassador in Germany (Attolico) was told by the German Foreign Ministry that there was nothing to stop Italy's assuming economic leadership in the Mediterranean area. But if it was a question of political leadership, Germany must come in. Hitler told Ciano on 1 October 1939 that the Duce could make a great contribution by rallying the neutral world under him. Mussolini, although he believed that the Balkan capitals would welcome the idea, rejected it. He had more dynamic plans. Ciano recorded that Hitler seemed tired, yet he spoke for almost two hours and cited figure after figure without referring to a single note. Ciano thought that he was either bewitched, or a genius. 'He outlines plans of action and cites dates with an assurance that does not admit of contradiction. Will he be proved right? In my opinion the game will not be as simple as he believes.'[19]

In the months before the ambitions of Hungary and Bulgaria led them to the brink of war with Romania, Hitler never lost an opportunity of reminding the Italians of the need for peace in the Balkans. When Count

[19] Ciano, p. 162.

Magistrati, the Italian Minister, called on him on 2 February 1940, on the eve of his transfer to Bulgaria, the Führer told him that the Balkans must remain completely still. If Hungary tried to recover Transylvania from Romania by force she might touch off a spark that would set the whole peninsula aflame. Romania too would do well to keep quiet, for once the fire broke out the Balkan powers would destroy each other; and it would be impossible to keep out Russia, Turkey, and other powers. He repeated this warning in a letter which Ribbentrop delivered to Mussolini on 10 March 1940. He wrote that he was glad to learn that Ciano was encouraging the Hungarians to defer their revisionist demands. If *any* country sought a revision of its boundaries it would light a fire that could not be contained. Neither Germany nor Italy wanted this. When Mussolini discussed the Balkans with Ribbentrop the following day he made it clear that he entirely agreed with Hitler's position.

He confirmed this in a letter to the Führer in which he drew attention to the situation in the Balkans and in particular to the ambiguous attitude of Romania, which had accepted an Anglo-French guarantee. He believed that it was in their common interest that this part of Europe should not become involved in war. In his reply a week later Hitler agreed that Romanian neutrality was dangerous, and said yet again the war must be kept from the Balkans. He then went on to reveal his feelings about these tiresome states which caused trouble out of proportion to their importance. When he had been fighting for power in Germany his most vile enemies were the unprincipled parties of bourgeois economic origin who were just like those little neutral states which insisted on the privilege of seriously offending and damaging, or at least threatening insolently some great powers which neglected them. This they excused by invoking the democratic freedom of the press and of public opinion. If anything was said or written that did not suit the leaders of these little nations they had many ways of exercising their influence and even imposing their veto.

Greece 1940-1941

Shortly after this, however, towards the end of April, the Führer seemed to shift his ground. He expressly authorized the German Ambassador in Italy

> To tell the Duce that the Führer would have no objection to the Duce's improving his strategic position, should he consider this necessary or desirable, very much as the Führer had done in the case of Denmark and Norway.

Mussolini heard this with obvious pleasure and remarked 'Very important', which Ciano echoed.[20]

This was a most important concession for it virtually gave Mussolini his head in the Balkans. It is difficult to understand why Hitler made it. He may have thought that he had warned his partner so often about the need for letting sleeping dogs lie that he would not dare to stir up trouble: or perhaps at this point of time he felt so much in command of his destiny that not even the blundering ambitions of the Duce could harm him.

Whatever the reason, in May 1940 the Germans became seriously worried lest the Italians should attack Yugoslavia; and so also did the Yugoslavs. The Yugoslav Minister in Italy (Christic) called on Ciano on 29 May 'as pale as a ghost' to express concern about Italy's hostile attitude. He was told, somewhat cryptically, that when Italy entered the war against Britain and France she would do so by the front door and not by the back door. When Ciano passed this on to the German Ambassador he added that there was great agitation in Yugoslavia, but he had used his influence to calm it down.[21]

It was Greece, however, and not Yugoslavia that was to be Mussolini's victim. Ever since he had occupied Albania in April 1939 Greece had been living under the threat of an Italian attack from that country. Relations between Italy and Greece had their ups and downs, depending on the Duce's whim; but immediately after his troops were established in Albania he gave an assurance that he would respect Greek independence. This was repeated from time to time.

[20] *DGFP* ix, pp. 234-6.
[21] Ciano, p. 257.

On 30 May the Duce wrote to the Führer about his decision to enter the war – which could now be done safely, in view of the German success in France – adding that he considered it unnecessary to extend the conflict to the Danube Basin and the Balkans. He would make a statement to reassure the nations concerned. Three days later in another letter to Hitler he reaffirmed that he would make a speech a few hours after his declaration of war (now due on 10 June) in which he would give specific assurances to the Danube countries, and Greece and Turkey.

At the beginning of July, however, it became evident that Italy was spoiling for a fight with Greece. Ciano taxed her with breaches of neutrality which had enabled the British to carry out aerial attacks on Italian submarines. The Greek Minister in Italy (Politis) thought that there were three possible explanations of the Italian allegations. Italy might be seeking to justify an attack on Greece to which she was already committed. She might be trying to bully Greece into siding with the Axis powers. Or it might simply be a device to mask the incompetence of the Italian navy.[22]

Ciano raised the question of Greece and Yugoslavia on 7 July when he met Hitler in Berlin – 'calm and reserved, very reserved for a German who has won'.[23] He said that Italy was very dissatisfied with the behaviour of Greece. She was giving the British fleet so much support that it found the Greek ports almost like home. Moreover she was providing information to the British about Italian submarines in her waters, which had led to the loss of four. If Corfu became a British base the industrial area of northern Italy would again become vulnerable to attacks by the RAF. Therefore Italy considered it necessary that she should occupy the Greek Islands in the Ionian Sea, in particular Corfu. Hitler seems to have done no more than note what Ciano said on this subject.

As to Yugoslavia, Ciano claimed that he now had proof

[22] *White Book*, nos. 87, 88.
[23] Ciano, p. 275.

of her insincerity. Prince Paul was a slave of the British. While Italy had hitherto agreed with Germany that the Balkans should be left in peace, the Duce now considered that the Yugoslav question must be settled within the next month. It would be a unique opportunity for Italy, since after the armistice with France she had only one land frontier to defend. The time was ripe for reducing the size of the Yugoslav state, a typical Versailles creation, and hostile to Italy.

Hitler now weighed in with his usual line. The real question was whether it was a matter of indifference to Mussolini which country had possession of the Dardanelles and Constantinople. If Italy attacked Yugoslavia, Hungary would immediately fall on Romania since she would no longer have anything to fear from Yugoslavia. The Russians would then cross the Danube and join forces with Bulgaria before pushing on to the Dardanelles and Constantinople. Germany would suffer damage if the war swept over the Romanian oilfields, from which she was still importing 140,000 tons a month. Ciano admitted that Italy too was drawing nearly all her oil from Romania, and said that he would at once transmit to the Duce the Führer's misgivings about an attack on Yugoslavia. He himself fully agreed with the case put forward by Hitler and he was sure that Mussolini would do so too. Settling Italy's account with Yugoslavia could wait until Britain had been dealt with.

Encouraged by Ciano's apparent obedience Hitler proceeded to talk about the respective spheres of influence of Germany and Italy. The Mediterranean and the Adriatic belonged to Italy, and Germany fully recognized this. The Yugoslav problem must be solved along Italian lines – when the time came. He did not mention Greece but it seems certain that he was assuming that Mussolini would not embark on the solution of the Greek problem without Germany's blessing.[24]

In the meantime the Italians were evolving contingency

[24] *DGFP* x, pp. 147-55.
[25] T 821 127.

plans for the invasion of Greece and Yugoslavia.[25] In September 1939 the Duce had reckoned that Greece was too poor to be added to his empire, but circumstances had changed. He was becoming more and more convinced that he must achieve some military success in Europe to balance Hitler's conquests. It did not really matter what country he took on – all that he wanted was a simple conquest which skilful propaganda could dress up into a brilliant campaign. The choice lay between Yugoslavia and Greece, which had common frontiers with Albania. Yugoslavia was first on the Duce's list because of his special hatred for her; but she was uncomfortably near Romania and her oilfields, and the Führer's warnings not to lay hands on Yugoslavia had been very clear. There was a strategic case for an attack on Greece since Britain might use her to strengthen her position in the eastern Mediterranean. So Greece it must be.

On 12 August Mussolini conferred in Rome with Francesco Jacomoni, Governor of Albania, and Sebastiano Visconti Prasca, Commander-in-Chief there. He told them that he had it in mind to attack Greece towards the end of September. If Ciamuria and Corfu surrendered without fighting he would leave it at that. If there *was* resistance, it would be answered by full-scale invasion. His advisers said that an immediate attack – while the weather remained good and the Greeks were still unprepared – was bound to succeed; but the Duce refused to move until later in the year.[26]

Round about this time there was a violent campaign in the government-controlled Italian press in support of Albania's claim to Epirus and Western Macedonia. Although the countries were officially at peace an Italian submarine torpedoed the Greek cruiser *Helle* while she was at anchor off the Island of Tenos, taking part in the celebration of the Feast of the Assumption. In spite of this extreme provocation Greece continued to maintain her position of strict neutrality.[27]

[26] Ciano, p. 283.
[27] *White Book*, nos. 87, 88.

From this time onwards it was obvious to the Germans that the Duce was up to something, and their numerous representatives in Rome did their best to find out what it was. Their Military Attaché (Rintelen) reported on 9 August a conversation with General Roatta, Deputy Chief of the Italian Army General Staff, about preparations for an Italian attack on Yugoslavia. Rintelen reminded Roatta that peace in the Balkans was essential for both the Axis partners. Roatta agreed, and said that they were only preparing for an operation that *might* become necessary, on instructions from their political leaders. Ten days later Ciano assured the German Ambassador that Italy planned no military action against Yugoslavia.[28]

The Greeks, no less than the Yugoslavs, were aware of the danger in which they stood. On 12 August Metaxas told the German Minister in Athens (Erbach) that he believed an Italian attack was imminent. Next day the Greek Minister in Berlin called on the State Secretary (Weizsäcker) to deny the report that an Albanian patriot had been killed by the Greeks – the main item in the trumped-up Italian press campaign. He went on to say that Greece had striven to remain neutral – yet the Italian air force had bombed her naval vessels on three separate occasions. Weizsäcker simply said that Germany trusted the reports of her ally; and rejected Rizo-Rangabé's request that the German press should publish the truth about the death of the Albanian – a brigand who had got his just deserts.[29]

German suspicions that Italy was about to attempt something increased as time went on. On 16 August Ribbentrop warned the Italian Ambassador (Alfieri) that Mussolini must attack neither Greece nor Yugoslavia. He would find it difficult to crush the Serbs who were good soldiers and would be helped by British bombers. The Ambassador later confirmed in writing that Italy planned nothing against Yugoslavia, and that the controversy with Greece was being moved on to the diplomatic plane. Ciano

[28] *DGFP* x, pp. 481-3, 513.
[29] *Ibid.* pp. 471-2.

30

repeated this in Rome next day to the German Ambassador. The Greek problem would be settled by diplomatic means. Italy would do nothing without first consulting Germany.[30]

The Greek Minister in Italy told Athens about this assurance which he distrusted on principle. It was much too like those which the Italians gave to Albania a few hours before they occupied *that* country. It showed, however, that the Axis partners were not working together, and that Germany suspected that Italy was about to use force. But the Germans could not stop the Italians, who badly needed an outstanding success. Therefore an Italian attack on Greece was possible at any moment.[31]

On 26 August, Ribbentrop, sensing no doubt that Mussolini was bent on aggression, made an attempt to spike his guns by winning Greece over to the side of the Axis. He summoned the Greek Minister and told him that his country had made a serious mistake by going over to Britain. For the coming centuries Europe would be controlled by the Axis powers whose relations with individual states would depend on their behaviour in the present struggle. The Mediterranean sphere belonged to Italy. Germany had no direct interest there. He advised Greece to remedy Italy's grievances – but Germany had no intention of intervening. Agreement with Italy was not impossible if Greece adopted the proper attitude. At the end of the meeting Rizo-Rangabé said that he was absolutely convinced that Germany would triumph over Britain. He for his part would do everything in his power to influence his government to get their policy on the right lines.

Ribbentrop met Mussolini and Ciano in Rome on 19 September, and once again warned them to keep their hands off Greece and Yugoslavia – at least for the time being. He was in great good humour and according to Ciano delighted with the welcome 'given him by "the applauding squad" which was very well mobilized by the

[30] *DGFP* x, pp. 495-8, 501-2.
[31] *White Book*, no. 135.

police commissioner'.[32] He began by making a comprehensive exposition of the war situation. England was on her knees. London would be reduced to ashes. Britain was staging the biggest bluff in her history. The RAF was steadily weakening. If only the weather had been better the war would now be over. After much more in the same vein he turned to Greece and Yugoslavia. Possibly carried away by the conviction that for all practical purposes the war was over, he said that the fate of these countries must be settled by Italy and by Italy alone; but it would be better to forget about them for the time being. The entire Axis effort must be concentrated on the destruction of Britain. As usual, Mussolini dutifully echoed the view of the senior partner. The war against Britain was the principal matter. Italy would not proceed against Greece and Yugoslavia right away. First of all she would conquer Egypt.[33]

During this time the planning of operations against Greece (*'Emergenza G'*) and Yugoslavia (*'Emergenza E'*) was being assiduously carried out by the Italian General Staff. Ciano first contemplated an attack on Greece during a visit to Albania in May 1940. He summoned General Carlo Geloso, commander of the army of occupation, and cross-examined him about the relative strength of the Greek and Yugoslav armies and the Italian forces in Albania. He then said that it was probable that a campaign would be undertaken against Greece within two or three weeks. Geloso was shocked, partly because this ran counter to all earlier directives, and partly because the Italian troops were in no position to mount an attack so soon, given the poor port facilities and the absence of good roads in Albania.[34]

An Italian dossier dated 11 September shows that as far as Greece was concerned it was proposed that there should be a major assault against Janina and Arta in Epirus, with a secondary attack on Philiates and Preveza. The forces engaged would join up in the region of Arta;

[32] Ciano, p. 291.
[33] *DGFP* xi, pp. 113-23.
[34] T 821 127/171-2.

and when this had been done, Corfu, Cephalonia and some other Ionian islands would be occupied. There was to be a demonstration against Macedonia to protect the left flank of the forces advancing on Arta and Preveza.[35]

On 29 September Ciano talked 'in rather vehement terms' about the Greeks in a meeting with Weizsäcker, who reminded him that it had been agreed that the Greek issue was of no importance at that moment. Ciano insisted, however, that something must be done to prevent the British fleet from finding sanctuary in the Greek Islands, should they be driven from Egypt. Nevertheless, when Hitler and Mussolini met at the Brenner Pass on 4 October there was no reference to the Balkans – at least so far as the German record goes. Hitler followed the line taken a fortnight earlier by his Foreign Minister. Britain was finished. Her last hopes were pinned on Russia and the United States. Both would let her down. He described at length, no doubt with relish, the preparations he had made for the final destruction of the British, who would have already been finished off if only their weather had been reasonable. Mussolini, as usual, agreed with everything his master said.[36] Ciano recorded 'rarely have I seen the Duce in such good humour and good shape'. Hitler 'put at least some of his cards on the table, and talked to us about his plans for the future . . .'[37]

Mussolini avoided Greece at the Brenner meeting; and Mackensen, the German Ambassador in Italy, reported on 18 October that Italian officials were also keeping off the subject. He believed that a show down was imminent. Jacomoni and Visconti Prasca, both of whom were supposed to favour action against Greece, had been summoned from Albania by Ciano. In passing on to Berlin the picture provided by his informant Mackensen said that all three agreed that precious time had been lost. A month or two earlier invasion would have been easy enough, but Marshal Badoglio, Chief of the Armed Forces General Staff, had

[35] T 821 127/203-6.
[36] *DGFP* xi, pp. 229, 245-9.
[37] Ciano, p. 296.

been against it. There were now strong Greek forces on the Albanian border. The final decision rested, of course, with Mussolini, who as far as Mackensen could judge shared Badoglio's view rather than Ciano's – although he could always change his mind. The Ambassador thought, however, that there was still reason to believe that the Duce would not seek to dispose of Greece until the power of Britain had been broken.

This report was off the mark in several respects. When Ciano had seen Badoglio the day before he was told that the General Staff were unanimously against action in Greece. For one thing they had too few men in Albania. Ciano argued that the moment was politically opportune. Neither Turkey nor Yugoslavia would lift a finger to help Greece. If Bulgaria came in it would be on the side of Italy. Secondly, there were no strong Greek forces on the Albanian border. Thirdly, and most important, Mussolini had irrevocably decided to invade Greece.

The ostensible reason, or justification, was Germany's action in sending forces to Romania without even telling him; and this at least Mackensen got right in his despatch of 18 October, in which he referred to 'the desire to make up in the popular mind for the loss of prestige which, as many people here believe, Italy has suffered as a result of her nonparticipation in the sending of military forces to Rumania'.[38] Ciano had written in his *Diary* on 12 October that above all Mussolini was indignant at the German occupation of Romania. The Duce said: 'Hitler always faces me with a fait accompli. This time I am going to pay him back in his own coin. He will find from the newspapers that I have occupied Greece. In this way the equilibrium will be re-established.'[39]

Now the German Foreign Ministry began to be alarmed. It was no longer safe to give the Italians their head. A telegram from the German liaison staff with the Italian air force led Karl Ritter, Ambassador with special duties in the Foreign Ministry, to draft a strong telegram to the

[38] *DGFP* xi, p. 323.
[39] Ciano, p. 297.

Italian government. The draft has not survived, but it must have urged Mussolini in very firm terms not to move against Greece. When Ribbentrop saw it he said it was too fierce. He suggested that instead 'a friendly question' should be put to the Italians. Before this could be done, however, Mackensen reported – on 19 October – that officers close to the Ministry of War were giving 23 October as the date for an operation against Greece, with Athens and Salonika as the primary objectives. He also referred to a conversation with Ciano who said that Greece's unneutral attitude must not continue indefinitely. When Mackensen asked in diplomatic language if this meant that Italy was going to invade Greece, Ciano simply shrugged his shoulders and replied that the Führer had conceded that Italy was free to do anything she pleased about Greece.[40]

As soon as Ribbentrop became aware of this exchange he ordered that 'the friendly question' should be held up. The matter must now be referred to the Führer himself. This was done, and Hitler decided that no question need be addressed to the Duce. He was due to see him shortly, and no doubt he assumed that his plans for an invasion of Greece would be tabled at their meeting, when he, the Führer, would once again see to it that they were shelved.[41]

On 19 October Mussolini drafted a letter to Hitler ostensibly to follow up matters they had considered on 4 October at the Brenner Pass. Greece figured prominently in spite of the fact that it had apparently not been discussed at the Brenner. The political classes there were pro-British, and the ordinary people had been trained to hate the Italians. Greece was to the Mediterranean what Norway was to the North Sea, and she must not escape the same fate. In making the last point he picked up Hitler's ill-advised suggestion made in April 1940 that there was no objection to the Duce's improving his strategic position in the Mediterranean, as he himself had done in Denmark and Norway. Much logistical effort –

[40] *DGFP* xi, pp. 326-7.
[41] *Ibid.* pp. 496-7.

comparable to the German preparations for the invasion of Britain – would be needed before they could resume the attack on Egypt, but he nevertheless hoped to launch simultaneous attacks on the Greek and Egyptian fronts. Mersa Matruh would be captured. It would then remain only to undertake the decisive battle of the Delta, in which German armoured support would be needed.

The despatch of this letter was held up, almost certainly deliberately. Although it was dated 19 October it was still being discussed in Rome on 22 October. Ciano recorded on that date: 'He alludes to our impending action in Greece but does not make clear either the form or the date, because he fears that once again an order might come to halt us. Many indications lead us to believe that in Berlin they are not very enthusiastic about our going to Athens.'[42]

The German team in Rome continued desperately to try to find out what the Italians' intentions really were. On 23 October Rintelen asked Roatta point blank whether the reinforcement of the Italian air force in Albania meant an early assault on Greece. Roatta dismissed the whole thing as a rumour. There was no intention whatever of taking military action against Greece.[43] The German Naval Attaché (Löwisch) reported independently that there would shortly be a surprise attack on Greece. Some of the Greek Islands would be occupied, but not Crete. There would be a simultaneous drive on Mersa Matruh.[44] By now it was widely assumed in all circles in Rome that the decision to attack had already been taken. The Greek Minister told Athens that rumours about the impending invasion continued unabated. It was expected that it would take place between 25 and 28 October.[45]

Badoglio told Rintelen on 24 October that while preparations had been completed for an offensive against Greece it was only a precautionary measure lest the British

[42] Ciano, p. 300.
[43] MOD 50/769.
[44] *Ibid.* 578/139.
[45] *White Book*, no. 168.

should violate Greek neutrality. In passing this on to
Berlin the Military Attaché said that the Italians were
concentrating all their efforts on Greece, and were pursu-
ing the war in Egypt with little energy. He thought they
would soon find an excuse to occupy Greece from Albania.
It was difficult to foresee the effect on the strategic balance
in the region. War in the Balkans would pull British troops
from North Africa, and might conceivably lead to a
German attack on Egypt from the east. The Bulgarians
would make no objection to the passage of German troops,
and a right of way could be achieved by force through
Turkey and Syria.[46]

Colonel General Franz Halder, Chief of the German
Army General Staff, recorded in his War Diary – also on
24 October – that Ciano was again busying himself with
the idea of occupying Corfu and the Greek mainland in
the neighbourhood of that Island. Hitler had stressed
repeatedly that the war strategy in the eastern Mediterranean would be quickly successful if Crete were occupied;
but it was madness to occupy the mainland of Greece.
The Führer was going to write to the Duce about the folly
of his plan.[47]

It was not until nine o'clock on the evening of 27
October – six hours before the Italian ultimatum to
Greece was due to be handed over, and eight and a half
hours before the Italian troops in Albania actually crossed
the Greek frontier – that Ciano summoned the German
Chargé d'Affaires (Bismarck) to tell him of Mussolini's
decision. The reason given for the invasion was Greece's
unneutral conduct in providing naval and air bases for the
British. The intention was to occupy Athens, Salonika,
and Lepanto. Just when this programme would be completed would depend on the course of the military operations – a wise rider, as it turned out. This time Hitler had
no chance to veto the enterprise. For once Mussolini had
left his partner standing at the post.[48]

[46] MOD 50/782-4.
[47] Franz Halder, *Kriegstagebuch*, vol. ii, p. 148.
[48] *DGFP* xi, p. 408.

That is, if they did not have a secret understanding, a possibility suggested by one authority.[49] The argument is that they may have had an off-the-record and private discussion at their Brenner meeting on 4 October (which is possible since the formal record of such a meeting is rarely comprehensive, and officials may not necessarily be informed about exchanges, for example, at a tête-à-tête luncheon); that on the eve of his journey to France and Spain which preceded the dictators' meeting at Florence on 28 October, and on the actual journey, Hitler was unmoved by numerous reports from German representatives in Rome and elsewhere that Italy was about to attack Greece, which led the High Command to believe that he must have given the Duce the green light; that his real purpose when he went to Florence 'was to talk Mussolini into co-operation with France, not to talk him out of his attack on Greece'; and that his outburst of anger when he learned on his special train that the attack had actually started (which was directed not against the Duce, but against Germany's representatives abroad for failing to keep him properly informed) was an act for the benefit of his immediate advisers designed to create an 'alibi' for himself in the event that the Italian attack, at which he had secretly connived, turned out to be a failure.

This is an interesting and well-documented theory which deserves serious study; but it is not claimed by its proponents to be the final word on the subject. It brings in the suggestion that Hitler was a good enough actor to put on a show of anger on the special train which deceived his entourage. If, however, his presumed acting ability is to be accepted as good evidence it can equally well be argued that his rage on first hearing the news of the invasion of Greece was the genuine article; and that it was his cordial greeting of Mussolini at Florence that was a piece of acting calling for all his histrionic talent. Again, if it is to be presumed that there was a secret exchange between the two dictators at the Brenner, it is equally

[49] Martin van Creveld, *Hitler's Strategy 1940-41: the Balkan Clue* (Cambridge, 1973), Ch. 2.

possible that in Florence there was a secret exchange to supplement the negligible discussion of the attack on Greece which took place at the conference table and was duly recorded.

The present writer, however, believes that the verdict about the secret understanding must for the time being remain 'not proven'. Hitler probably hoped to continue to restrain his partner from attacking Greece, in spite of the reports which had been coming in, and it may simply have been the realization of his error of judgement that drove him to fury on the special train. That he refrained from castigating the Duce at Florence may have been due to the fact that there was always the possibility that the Italian invasion of Greece would turn out to be the triumphal procession which its sponsors hoped it would be; and he would have to eat his words before many days had passed.

For the whole of the last year Hitler had succeeded against heavy odds in keeping the Balkans at peace. Now, with or without his connivance, his ally had put at risk the fruits of many months of difficult diplomatic negotiation. At the Florence meeting the Führer merely said that Germany could make available for the military operations against Greece, especially to keep out the British, a division of airborne troops and a division of paratroops. Mussolini said nothing at all.[50] His silence would have been even more understandable a few days later when it had become apparent that he had bitten off more than he could chew.

[50] *DGFP* xi, pp. 411-22; Halder, p. 157.

II

1. Mussolini uncontrolled: the invasion of Greece

For the purposes of their defence the Greeks had divided the territory facing the Albanian border into two sectors, one running west from Mount Smolikas to the Ionian Sea, containing Epirus and Pindus and covering the towns of Amphilochia and Metsovon; and the other running east from Mount Smolikas to Lake Prespa, containing Western Macedonia and covering the towns of Florina and Salonika.

They had, of course, also to guard their other frontiers, and here the shape of the country put them at a serious disadvantage. Although the heart of the Greek mainland – bounded by the Ionian Sea in the west, the Aegean in the east and the Gulf of Corinth in the south, is reasonably compact, the northern areas are the opposite. The frontier straggles from the west along Albania, Yugoslavia, Bulgaria, and finally Turkey. Its total length is about 600 miles, compared with only 130 miles for a line drawn across the mainland from the Ionian to the Aegean Sea, not many miles further south. In 1940 there was no immediate danger from Yugoslavia or Turkey, but there was every likelihood of an attack from Albania, where a frontier of 140 miles had to be defended; and there was a possible threat from Bulgaria, more than a hundred miles to the east, where the common frontier was 250 miles long.

The Greeks therefore might have to spread their forces over two long fronts many miles distant from each other. They planned to allocate 8 infantry divisions and two infantry brigades to the Albanian theatre; and 6 infantry divisions and one infantry brigade to the Bulgarian. Their reserves were to be maintained in the Salonika area from which they could move relatively easily to both theatres.

Although they began to mobilize in August, urged on

by the reports of their Minister in Rome,[1] they made no attempt to put substantial forces on the Albanian frontier since that would provide a ready-made excuse for an Italian attack, the border area having been demilitarized since September 1939. They accepted that the main battle would have to be joined well within Greek territory; but at least this would give them time to determine where the most serious threat was developing. General Papagos, the Greek Commander-in-Chief, had no doubt about the wisdom of this. In his own account of these events he wrote: 'Accordingly, it was laid down that even at the cost of national territory the defensive battle would have to be given before those positions where it would be possible to ensure the concentration of the allocated Greek forces.'[2] A stand would be made either at a line about a dozen miles from the frontier – if the overwhelming superiority of the Italians in the air, and the difficulty of movement in the mountains, allowed it;[3] or at a line fifteen to twenty miles further back ('the minimum line of resistance');[4] or somewhere between these two lines.

The Italians attacked at 5.30 on the morning of 28 October, half an hour before their ultimatum expired; but this breach of etiquette was so small in relation to the infamy of their whole position vis-à-vis the Greeks that it hardly mattered. The latter had only minor defence works in the border passes, where they hoped to fight delaying actions to give their main forces time to assemble further back; and sheer weight of numbers enabled the Italians to make headway through most difficult mountain country, in spite of the atrocious weather conditions. Mussolini could not have chosen a worse time of year to invade. Flying in the mountains – hazardous enough in the best

[1] e.g. *White Book*, no. 135.
[2] A. Papagos, *The Battle of Greece*, p. 239.
[3] Lemos, Mount Varmba, Mount Flatsata, Mount Psoriaka, Mount Stavros, Mount Smolikas, Mount Gamila, Elea, (Kalpaki), Kalamas River.
[4] Kaimaktsalan, Mount Vermion, Hadova Pass, Porta Pass, Aliakmon River, Venetikos River, Mount Orliakas, Zigos, Metsovon, Arachthos River.

of circumstances – was at first impossible because of the constant storms, which meant that for two or three days the advancing troops were completely without air support.[5] For the same reason only limited artillery support was possible. Rivers were swollen by the torrential rain – the Kalamas at the point where the Italians crossed was sixty metres wide instead of the usual twenty; and all through the Italian Commander-in-Chief's initial reports it is clear that it was the weather as much as the Greek forces that provided the opposition.[5]

Nevertheless this did not inhibit Visconti Prasca from sending back to Rome enthusiastic praise for the wonderful spirit of his troops, who were superior to the enemy in every respect – if his assessment is to be believed. In fact, the engagements in the first four days, while the Italians were moving through lightly-defended territory, were relatively minor. Over the whole front they lost only six officers and five men killed, and 217 men wounded; and they captured only thirty-five prisoners.[6]

The Italian plan of attack was broadly on the lines contemplated by their General Staff in September, except that initially it was confined to the mainland.[7] There was to be no attempt to move against Western Macedonia in the sector between Mount Grammos and Lake Prespa, but there were to be three separate attacks against Epirus and Pindus between Mount Grammos and the Ionian Sea. The major effort, in the centre, was to be directed against the town of Janina. A secondary thrust – north of Koritsa, aimed at Metsovon – was intended to cut the Greek communication lines between Epirus and Thessaly. Thirdly, a force was to make its way along the coast through Philiates and across the Kalamas River, with the town of Arta as its ultimate objective. Finally, as soon as reasonable progress had been made on the mainland, the Island of Corfu was to be occupied.

The main attack was launched from the valleys of the

[5] T 821 127/101, 551-9.
[6] *Ibid.* 558.
[7] See above, pp. 32-3.

Rivers Drin and Vijose in Albania. The primary objective in this sector was the town of Kalpaki, where there was an important crossroads, from which it was intended to drive on Janina, and thence to Arta. The Italians had little difficulty in disposing of the light Greek forces in the border area and reached Kalpaki on 29 October. Here they paused to reorganize. By 2 November they had occupied the Grambala height to the north of the town; but this was to be the limit of their progress in the central front. On 3 November they were driven back by a Greek counter-attack, recaptured the position on the 8th, and were then immediately driven out again. The central thrust, on which their main hopes were pinned, had come to nothing. On 9 November they tried in vain to win back the Grambala height. Thereafter there was no further assault in this sector, although the artillery and air force continued to be active.[8]

The attack by the Italian left wing, which had Metsovon as its objective, took the invaders between Mount Grammos and Mount Gamila through the valleys of the Kerasovitikos and the Aoos Rivers; and here they made better progress. They captured the village of Vovoussa – their deepest penetration into Greek territory – and got within striking distance of Metsovon. It had, however, become obvious to the Greeks shortly after the invasion began that the enemy had no intention of going for Western Macedonia, which would have involved them in fighting on a much wider front. The Greek High Command therefore took the offensive in this region, where the Italians were presumably less strong, to create a diversion and relieve their forces on the other fronts.

The Italian right wing, attacking from Konispol on the Albanian border, captured the town of Philiates, and on 5 November bridged the Kalamas, in spite of heavy rain. In the evening the Greeks destroyed the newly-erected bridge. It was quickly repositioned, however, and next day the Italians established a substantial bridgehead. They

[8] T 821 127.

then advanced along the coast and occupied Igoumenitsa on 6 November. According to Papagos the small Greek forces were forced to fall back 'in a more or less disorderly manner' and finally regrouped on the Acheron River marshes, where it had been planned to make a stand.[9]

It became obvious to the Italian General Staff soon after the invasion began that things were not going to plan. Badoglio sent a message to Visconti Prasca, speaking 'as his former superior'. He directed that the Commander-in-Chief should solidly anchor his troops in one place – which must be the Koritsa sector, on the left of the Italian line. In that area he had the Parma and Piemonte Divisions, and very soon the Venezia Division would arrive. The Bari Division, which had been earmarked for the proposed occupation of Corfu – called off on 2 November when it had become apparent that there was no question of simply walking into Greece; and the Arrezzo Division might also be available.[10] Five divisions must surely be enough to stabilize the front.

On 4 November Visconti Prasca thanked Badoglio – 'always my master' – for his guidance, and agreed that he read the situation exactly as the Field Marshal had done. In the circumstances he could hardly have done otherwise. He said that at first the situation in the Koritsa sector had been extremely delicate, when only the Parma Division was available, but it had improved after the arrival of the Venezia and Piemonte Divisions, which for lack of motor transport had had to march for two and three weeks respectively through very difficult country. He concluded that the situation was no longer disquieting and asserted his faith in the final outcome. The initial difficulties were due simply to inadequate transport and bad weather.[11]

Bulgaria's attitude was uncertain when the Italians began the invasion, for it had been impossible – because of Mussolini's anxiety to keep his plans secret – to sound out any country. The Italians wanted a swift and easy

[9] Papagos, p. 266.
[10] T 821 127/98.
[11] *Ibid.* 98.

passage into Greece before the Bulgarians had time to consider whether they should try to seize part of the spoils. Moreover, if Bulgaria came in the glory of the Duce's triumph would be tarnished. When the Greek High Command saw that the Bulgarians were not going to move they transferred part of their forces watching the Bulgarian frontier to strengthen their western front. The Italian General Staff estimated, with apprehension, that Bulgaria's negative attitude would allow Greece to move at least three divisions to Western Macedonia and seriously to threaten the Italian left wing.[12]

The Greeks also brought up the reserves held in the neighbourhood of Salonika since it was now unlikely that they would be needed to stem a Bulgarian attack. Their plan was to give first priority to the protection of Thessaly – even if it meant sacrificing the coastal area between Philiates and Arta. According to Papagos: 'In this case the loss of national territory would not be quite so serious as the cutting of the communications of the Epirus forces with Thessaly and the forcing by the invader of the gates to Southern Greece.'[13]

Less than a fortnight after the Italians had launched their attack the main Greek forces were in position in Epirus and Pindus. The invaders were brought to a sudden halt. Almost immediately the Greeks began to force them back; and by the evening of 13 November they had swept them from all Greek territory north and north-west of Mount Smolikas, and had gained control of the main frontier crossings. In Papagos's view this was the more remarkable since it was accomplished by troops which had only just been mobilized and had no real experience in the field. Further, they had to rely on women and children to help to move their supplies in mountainous country where ordinary vehicles could not operate. To the west, where the Italians had decided not to invade, Greek troops from Western Macedonia established themselves in Albania in the valley of the upper Devoli River.

[12] T 821 127/94.
[13] Papagos, p. 262.

A week later the Greek High Command decided to carry the war into enemy territory. They planned that their troops from Western Macedonia should occupy the Morova heights in Albania and move against the important junction at Koritsa. Thereafter they would swing round towards Ereska and Leskovic. The forces based on Janina would also aim for Koritsa. The counter-offensive would start on 14 November, in spite of the fact that all the necessary forces could not be concentrated by that date: but speed was of the essence, to make the best use of the men while they were still elated by their initial successes, and to forestall the arrival of Italian reserves.

2. Italian failure: November-December 1940

The counter-offensive began at dawn on 14 November. It was intended to give the impression that the whole front from Lake Prespa to the Ionian Sea was being attacked, so that at first the true objectives would be concealed. The real purpose was to push the Italians back along the three main routes by which they had entered Greece; and for good measure to mount a major offensive from Western Macedonia towards the Morova heights in Albania, where there had been relatively little activity, and where the divisions brought from the Bulgarian frontier could play their part.

The attack on the Morova heights was launched between Mount Grammos and Lake Prespa through mountainous terrain where the Italian tanks found it difficult to operate effectively. This was the more necessary since the Greeks had no tanks and virtually no anti-tank weapons. By 22 November the Greeks, after some stiff fighting in which the Italian air force played a greater part than hitherto, had occupied the whole of the Morova heights and had taken the town of Koritsa.[14] They then set about consolidating a deep protective zone to the north and south of the River Devoli, and drove the Italians back to

[14] WO 201/11.

Pogradec. The Italians established new defensive positions south of the town, but were driven out on 30 November. By 8 December the Greeks were firmly in command of the region, well-placed to frustrate any Italian attempt to resume the offensive.

They attacked in Epirus from the Kalpaki sector, also on 14 November. It was mainly in this sector that their troops had been inadequately reinforced, but the Greek High Command took a chance in the hope of convincing the enemy that they were able to attack along the whole length of the frontier. The gamble came off. The initial assault made good progress, and when the reinforcements arrived on 17 November, after long and exhausting marches, they threw themselves on the Italians with great *élan*. By 22 November they had driven them out, and were established on the Albanian border to the west of the Aoos River.

The advance along the Ionian coast began on 12 November. Igoumenitsa was captured on the 17th and the Italians were pushed back to the River Kalamas. Three days later the Greeks crossed the river and on 22 November recaptured Philiates, whereupon the Italians withdrew to the border.

The enemy had been cleared from Greek soil remarkably quickly, despite their superior equipment and an air force which was unopposed. In Albania the Greeks had won the Morova heights and Pogradec. They had captured Koritsa and Leskovic, and with them control of the highway between Koritsa and Merdjan, which made it easy to switch their forces from north to south.

The High Command could now contemplate building on these initial successes. It was decided that the forces from Western Macedonia must continue to protect the Koritsa heights and harass the enemy facing them to reduce pressure on the Greeks further south. It was hoped to advance in the centre towards Berat, across the valley of the Aoos River. On the left they would move towards Argyrokastron with the ultimate objective of capturing the Albanian seaport of Valona.

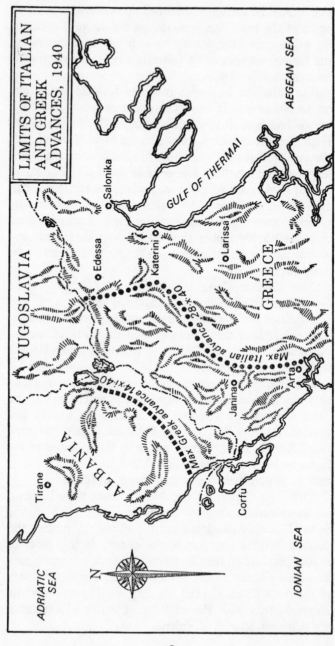

LIMITS OF ITALIAN
AND GREEK
ADVANCES, 1940

YUGOSLAVIA

ALBANIA

Tirane

GREECE

AEGEAN
SEA

GULF OF THERMAI

Salonika

Edessa

Katerini

Larissa

Max. Italian advance 28.x.40

Max. Greek advance 14.xi.40

Janina

Arta

Corfu

ADRIATIC
SEA

IONIAN SEA

N

The Italians' optimism about the success of their invasion, and the dire trouble in which they had landed themselves, are clearly illustrated by their memoranda and operational orders. A memorandum by General Soddu dated 27 November reviewing the first month of the war reveals the sorry state of the Italian forces and their command. It refers to events and mental attitudes which must at all costs be avoided in future. The invasion had been undertaken in the firm conviction, shared by all, that the Greeks had no genuine military ability and that the Italian troops would have to do no more than carry out a military parade. It was this that had led to their undoing. Now the pendulum had swung too far the other way. Soddu claimed that the Greeks, whose success was due simply to their skilful exploitation of Italian mistakes, were now just as much over-rated as they had at first been under-rated.

He had some pointed things to say about the performance of his troops in the field, and their commanders. Too often small units had called in aircraft to bomb Greek patrols which should have been disposed of instead by a vigorous infantry counter-attack. Many men had never set eyes on their commanding general. It was not enough just to issue orders. Commanders should personally ensure that they were carried out. A new spirit must be instilled in the troops. They must be taught to hate the Greeks, for example by propaganda based on the disgraceful treatment of Italian prisoners of war and 'acts of brigandage' against field hospitals – happily emotive subjects. The soldier must learn to consider himself superior to the enemy. A spirit of ardour and boldness must be cultivated in him. When all this had been done 'our magnificent soldiery' would overcome every obstacle, and victory would be theirs.[15]

The operational orders are equally revealing. *Direttiva No 1 per le operazioni contro la Grecia* was issued, not as might be expected on 28 October when they entered

[15] T 821 207/549-52.

Greece, but on 10 November when the campaign was nearly a fortnight old and was for the first time seen as a potential disaster. Subsequent *Direttive* were issued by Soddu only after an elaborate drafting process had been completed. This meant that when the orders reached the troops the military situation had as a rule changed greatly. The academic care with which Soddu sought the *mot juste* in successive drafts, at a time when his troops were being relentlessly thrown back, may have contributed to their failure to hold the Greeks.

Direttiva No 5, for example, the first draft of which is dated 2 December, bravely ignores the possibility of further retreat. The line must be held at whatever cost, and the defenders are required if necessary to face up to the supreme sacrifice. A subsequent draft, however, does envisage the regrettable eventuality that events may dictate a further retreat. After two more drafts had been prepared and extensively tinkered with, the order was finally issued on 4 December. The alarming reference to the supreme sacrifice was tactfully deleted, and the troops were now asked to do no more than defend their ground *metro per metro*. But it had taken so long to get the order out that Pogradec, which in the first draft had to be held to the last man, had to be omitted from the line of resistance – since it was now occupied by the Greeks.[16]

In spite of Soddu's sound advice and brave words, and possibly because of his carefully-drafted *Direttive*, the Italian retreat continued. On 28 December, however, the Greek High Command had to call a halt to enable them to consolidate the positions they had won. They also needed time to improve their communications and transport. The problems which the Italians had experienced in these fields applied no less to the Greeks. The further they penetrated into Albania the more difficult they became. Although they held a line running from Pogradec in the east to the Ionian Sea just north of Khimara, they could not get as far as Berat or Valona, mainly because of

[16] T 821 207/485-590.

Italian superiority in the air, and their lack of tanks and anti-tank weapons.

3. Playing from weakness: the British position

The British War Cabinet was, of course, deeply interested in events in the Balkans and their effect on the British position in the Mediterranean. When the Spanish Foreign Minister (Beigbeder) suggested that at their meeting at the Brenner Pass Hitler and Mussolini had agreed to launch an offensive against Egypt via Turkey (which they had not) the idea was immediately reported to London by the British Ambassador (Sir Samuel Hoare). On 9 October the War Cabinet tested the idea. The Germans were building aerodromes near the Romanian oilfields, which might be a prelude to the intimidation of Turkey. The Prime Minister said that if Germany threw her weight into an eastward thrust the countries in her path could do no more than delay her progress. At the end of the discussion the Chiefs of Staff were instructed to examine the possibility that the Germans would mount a campaign with the Persian Gulf or Suez Canal as their objective.[17]

In an earlier paper they had concluded that Germany would be forced to take further action after the fall of France, mainly because of her oil shortage, but that it was unlikely that she would attack any of the Balkan states. She might lose their raw materials in a general conflagration (curiously enough Hitler's favourite expression in the context of the Balkans). In the meantime, however, she had moved peacefully into Romania, thereby securing her oil supplies; but the Axis still needed raw materials from elsewhere in the Balkans, and on economic grounds would hesitate to disturb the peace there. The Prime Minister's off-the-cuff analysis was confirmed. Bulgaria could offer no resistance; Greece would be overwhelmed by a combined German Italian attack; an isolated Yugoslavia would be in no position to resist Axis demands. Syria could not

[17] CAB 65/15, f. 69.

be relied on to oppose the Nazis, while Iraq would welcome them with open arms. Turkey alone seemed likely
to put up a fight. Therefore every effort must be made to
induce Russia to support her; and Britain must also give
the Turks all the help in her power.[18] At the end of the
day, however, the War Cabinet concluded that the attack
on Egypt would come from the west.

The British were just as much aware of the rumours
that Italy was about to attack Greece as everybody else;
but they could get no confirmation – which was hardly
surprising when even the Germans remained in the dark,
despite the efforts of their many representatives in Rome.
On 28 October rumour gave place to hard fact. The
Cabinet reviewed the situation which Mussolini had
created, in order to determine how Britain could give
Greece the help she had pledged in April 1939.

Churchill and his colleagues in London had no doubt
that every effort must be made to help the Greeks. At this
time, however, the British Secretary of State for War
(Anthony Eden) was in Cairo for discussions with General
Wavell, Commander-in-Chief, Middle East. Eden and his
advisers in North Africa were equally certain that the
defence of Egypt must have the first priority, and that no
help could be spared for Greece. These diametrically
opposed views, and the thousands of miles between the
two men, gave rise to a curious exchange of telegrams.

On 1 November – four days after the invasion of
Greece began – Eden, influenced by his talks with Wavell,
got in an early blow by saying to Churchill that there was
no hope of sending enough support from North Africa to
have any real effect on events in Greece. To send *any*
men from Egypt would imperil the whole position in the
Middle East and jeopardize plans for offensive operations
now being laid in more than one theatre. This circum-
locution was a broad hint that Wavell was planning a
major offensive in the desert against the Italians. It could
be no more than a hint since Eden had deferred, wrongly,

---

[18] FO 371/24892, ff. 7-24.

it may be thought, to Wavell's insistence that no one, not even the Prime Minister, should be told of his plans. Eden went on to say that it would be bad strategy to split the British effort between the two theatres. The best way to help Greece was to hit Italy.[19]

Churchill seems to have missed the hint. His reply was instant and uncompromising. In his view the Greek situation dominated all others. Aid to Greece must be attentively studied lest the Turks, noting that Britain never kept her guarantees, were lost to the allied cause. He invited the Secretary of State to stay on in Cairo for at least a week while the position was examined.[20]

On 3 November the telegrams between the two men flew thick and fast. Each sent three, powerfully advancing his own reading of the situation. Eden said that everybody in Cairo was strongly of the opinion that he must come home as soon as possible in order to describe the position as seen from Egypt.[21] This time the Prime Minister replied, not with a polite invitation that Eden should remain in Cairo, but with a peremptory order beginning: 'Do not return . . .' He said it would be most unfortunate at this juncture if action were paralysed both in London and Egypt simply because the Secretary of State was in transit between the two places. He added pertinently that he did not understand why Eden could not telegraph the points he had in mind.[22]

Eden countered with a précis of his discussions with Wavell in which it had been accepted that Britain's policy towards Greece had been clearly laid down and communicated to the Greeks on several occasions. It had been decided that they could be given no help until the threat to Egypt had been finally liquidated. The security of Egypt was vital to British strategy, and incidentally to the future of Greece. It must take precedence over attempts to prevent Greece from being overrun.[23] Later in the day Eden

[19] PREM 3/308, ff. 23-6.
[20] *Ibid.* f. 110.
[21] *Ibid.* f. 19.
[22] *Ibid.* f. 108.
[23] *Ibid.* ff. 16-17.

sent another telegram dealing in more detail with the im-
possibility of providing help from North Africa. It was
assumed that the Greek army most needed anti-aircraft
and anti-tank guns, which were precisely the things that
were scarce in North Africa. At best no more than a
brigade could be spared for Greece – a drop in the ocean,
which would deprive the desert forces of their only
reserves. By dividing Britain's limited resources they
would risk failure both in the Western Desert and in
Greece.[24]

Still on 3 November the Prime Minister fired another
shot. The gravity and consequence of the Greek situation
compelled Eden's presence in Cairo. If Britain allowed
Greece to collapse without lifting a finger to help her it
would have a deadly effect on the Turks and the future
of the war. The Greeks were probably as good as the
Italians, and the Germans were not yet on the spot. If a
major offensive in Libya was not contemplated during the
next two months, then risks must be run to stimulate
Greek resistance. The minor offensives of which Eden had
spoken must take second place to effective action in
Greece. Churchill then let himself go:

> No-one will thank us for sitting tight in Egypt with ever-
> growing forces while Greek situation and all that hangs on
> it is cast away . . . Trust you will grasp situation firmly
> abandoning negative and passive policies and seizing oppor-
> tunity which has come into your hands. 'Safety first' is the
> road to ruin in war, even if you had the safety, which you
> have not. Send me your proposals earliest, or say you have
> none to make.[25]

Eden's third telegram of the day, in which he responded
to Churchill's peevish instruction, is the most interesting
in the series:

> Following for Prime Minister from Secretary of State for
> War:

> Entirely for your own information Wavell is having plans

[24] PREM 3/308, f. 15.
[25] *Ibid.* ff. 105-7.

prepared to strike blow against Italians in Western Desert at the earliest possible moment, probably this month. He is particularly anxious to keep secret his intention which is at present known only to very few senior commanders and staff officers who are drawing up plans. Plan involves certain risks and requires all trained and fully equipped troops in Western Desert and Reserve in Egypt. Margin is small and any withdrawal of troops or equipment would mean cancelling plan and remaining on defensive. It is of this plan that I wish to speak to you on my return.[26]

Eden had already hinted that something was afoot in the Western Desert, but out of deference to Wavell's wishes he had done no more than hint, and Churchill had not taken the point. Now, in this later telegram he spelled out why he and his advisers were so dead set against helping Greece; and he might reasonably have assumed that it would be crystal clear to the Prime Minister why he had seemed to be dragging his feet. Nevertheless, he writes in his memoirs, referring to the telegram immediately above: '. . . I telegraphed hinting, but not proclaiming, our plans . . .' Surely the words he actually used, that Wavell was 'having plans prepared to strike blow against Italians in Western Desert at the earliest possible moment, probably this month', taken in conjunction with the earlier hint about 'offensive operations now being laid', and Eden's earlier reluctance to allow a single gun or man to leave North Africa for Greece, added up to a full-blooded 'proclamation', the implications of which would leap to the eye of the dullest reader, and could hardly escape the Prime Minister, who was eagerly awaiting just such an announcement.

It is curious that Eden should describe a positive statement of a crucial fact as being no more than a hint. Further, although he quotes at length in his memoirs from others of his messages to the Prime Minister he does not quote from this, the most important.[27] Nor is it even mentioned by Churchill who, like Eden, quotes directly from

[26] PREM 3/308, f. 14.
[27] Anthony Eden, *Memoirs: The Reckoning*, p. 171.

many of the relevant telegrams. When Eden's messages were printed for the War Cabinet, Churchill instructed that those sent in their personal cipher should be omitted, which meant that his colleagues in the War Cabinet were unaware that a major assault was being planned in North Africa. Only Churchill, and General Ismay who *was* allowed to see the personal messages, knew the truth.[28]

When Eden arrived back in London on 8 November and sought out the Prime Minister 'after the usual air raid had begun' he 'brought with him the carefully-guarded secret which I [Churchill] had wished I had known earlier'. And again: 'Here, then, was the deadly secret which the Generals had talked over with their Secretary of State. This was why they had not wished to telegraph. We were all delighted. I purred like six cats. Here was something worth doing.'[29]

Why did Churchill wait until 8 November before allowing himself to purr like six cats? He knew five days earlier what was planned in North Africa. Why did he pretend that he did not? Why, nearly ten years later, when no security reason inhibited him from setting out the facts, did he tell his readers that he had to wait for Eden's return to learn that Wavell was about to mount an offensive? It looks like a deliberate attempt to conceal his knowledge of the proposed offensive both at the time, and when he was writing *The Second World War*; but if this is true it is difficult to understand what his purpose was. As Churchill himself recorded, however, the 'misunderstanding' – genuine or pretended – did no harm. In the end Britain gave Greece all the help she could reasonably expect, and the transfer of resources from North Africa did not affect Wavell's offensive.

So long as Eden remained in North Africa he continued to grumble about the claims of Greece. On 5 November he said that while the risks in providing her with aid must be accepted in view of Britain's political commitment, it

28 PREM 3/308, f. 6.
29 Churchill, vol. ii, pp. 479-80.

would be at the cost of additional risks and probably increased casualties in the Western Desert.[30] Next day he
telegraphed that the more he thought about sending help
to Greece the more it troubled him, particularly since it
was on the cards that the purpose of the Italian invasion
was to induce Britain to weaken her forces in North
Africa, the vital theatre of Europe.[31]

While Churchill was goading a seemingly-reluctant
Secretary of State for War and the Middle East Command
into striking in Greece while the iron was hot, he took it
upon himself to order aircraft from North Africa to
Greece. Air Chief Marshal Sir Arthur Longmore, in command of the RAF in the Middle East, had earlier said
that he was so short of modern aircraft that it was quite
out of the question to send any aeroplanes to the Greeks,
but an urgent appeal from the British Minister in Athens
(Sir Michael Palairet) after the Italian invasion made him
change his mind. He now considered that the Greeks must
be helped at all costs. On his own responsibility, without
the blessing of the Commander-in-Chief, Middle East
(perhaps because he knew that that blessing would not be
given) he sent a squadron of Blenheims. The Prime
Minister immediately signified his approval on 1 November by congratulating Longmore on his very bold and
wise decision, thereby stifling any adverse comment from
the other commanders in North Africa.[32]

Churchill told the War Cabinet on 4 November that
Britain could not afford the stigma of allowing yet another
small nation to be swallowed up. True, the French, who
were now out of the struggle, had been supposed to im-
plement the joint Anglo-French guarantee to Greece; but
the world would not forgive Britain if she did nothing. It
was only in the air, however, that speedy support could
be provided, which meant transferring precious aircraft
from Egypt. Without waiting to argue the merits of the
case with Middle East Command, or even to discuss them

[30] PREM 3/308, f. 12.
[31] *Ibid.* f. 89.
[32] *Ibid.* 309/1, f. 6.

with his Cabinet colleagues, he had ordered that in addition to the first squadron (Blenheim fighters and bombers) four more should go to Greece, two of Blenheims (bombers) and two of Gladiators (single-seat bi-plane fighters). The Foreign Secretary (Viscount Halifax) welcomed his decision. He was certain that to send no help would undermine the will to resist in all the other Balkan countries. The real problem, however, was how to put heart into Greece without revealing Britain's serious weakness in North Africa.[33]

The Greek government expressed their gratitude for Britain's prompt help through the King and Metaxas – although privately they thought it was too little and too slow in arriving. On 18 November they asked for more aircraft; but the War Cabinet decided that except for an additional twelve Gladiators for the use of the Greek air force no more could be sent. The Prime Minister chided the British Minister in Athens, who was pressing the Greek case, for failing to understand the practical difficulties of moving aircraft from one country to another, and therefore misleading his host government. Palairet had proposed a scheme for transferring Hurricanes, an up-to-date aircraft which in any case the British government had no intention of releasing to the Greeks for the time being, at short notice. With characteristic disregard for personal feelings Churchill ordered the Minister to summon his Air Attaché and ask him to explain the facts of life in this specialist field. Unreasonable and impossible requests must be stopped. As it was, the help given to Greece, totalling at that date seventy-four aircraft, would seriously deplete British strength in Egypt.[34]

This was painfully true. *Barbarity*, the code name used for the expedition, deprived the forces in Egypt of about half their operational aircraft until such time as reinforcements could be sent from Britain – a measure of the risk which the British had taken for the sake of their ally. The total strength of *Barbarity*, including army detachments

[33] CAB 65/16, f. 8.
[34] *Ibid.* f. 32.

to man the anti-aircraft defences of the aerodromes, and
the other ancillary services, amounted to about 5,000
men.[35]

It was not only aircraft that the Greeks lacked, however. They were short of almost everything, and what they
did have was largely out of date. Major-General T. G. G.
Heywood, head of the British military mission in Athens,
reported that all their field guns had been through every
campaign since 1912, and were almost worn out.[36] In
response to a request from the Greek Minister in London
(Simopoulos) who stressed the need for rifles, anti-aircraft
guns, and anti-tank guns, the Chiefs of Staff drew up a
list of equipment which Britain could spare. This provoked a scathing minute from the Prime Minister. He
wrote that the munitions which it was proposed to send
were very meagre, in most cases no more than one per
cent. of the supplies available, and sometimes even less
than that. No field guns were included, no anti-tank guns,
only eight heavy anti-aircraft guns out of 1,100 available
in Britain. He inevitably spotted that ammunition had not
been mentioned, and presumed with heavy sarcasm that
the Greeks *would* be given something to fire from any
guns that *were* sent. The whole matter must be re-
examined in the light of the achievements of the Greek
forces.

The list was hastily amended. Twenty-four 75-mm field
guns and twenty anti-tank rifles were added. The number
of 3.7 inch anti-aircraft guns was doubled to sixteen, and
Bofors were more than trebled from twelve to forty. Comparable increases were made in the other stores in the list;
and those concerned with compiling it – no doubt in-
furiated by the Prime Minister's ability to spot a weakness
in any paper that crossed his desk – dutifully added the
appropriate ammunition for every type of gun included.[37]

The first British planes reached Greece on 3 November.
They operated from Tatoi and Eleusis near Athens, under

[35] WO 201/2727.
[36] WO 201/11.
[37] FO 371/24916, ff. 122, 127.

the command of Air-Commodore John D'Albiac, and at once mounted a standing patrol over the capital which put heart into the Athenians. The Greek High Command asked that the British planes should provide close support for their forces in the field, but D'Albiac insisted that they should be employed in strategic bombing against Italian lines of communication and troop concentrations in back areas. He would allow them to give direct support to the land forces only if a critical situation developed. At least for the moment he had his way. His aircraft raided the harbours on the Albanian coast – Valona, Durazzo and Sarande; fuel dumps near the capital Tirane; and supply and communication centres at Tepelene, Argyrokastron, and Elbasan. Heavy bombers – Wellingtons – from Egypt, using an arming and refuelling base in Greece, added their weight to the squadrons which had been transferred from North Africa.[38]

It is difficult to evaluate the contribution made by the RAF in the first months. Some damage was done to ships, harbour installations and other targets, but it was impossible to interfere seriously with the movement of Italian reinforcements. The crossing from the heel of Italy was short enough to be completed within the hours of darkness, so that Italian troopships could be attacked only in the ports, which were well defended. On paper the RAF did well enough. On one occasion a Gladiator patrol shot down seven Italian fighters for the loss of only one of their own, which collided with and destroyed an eighth Italian fighter. On another, nine Gladiators took on six bombers and fifty fighters. They reported eight enemy fighters shot down for the loss of two Gladiators. But the British squadrons, which were stretched to the utmost and often had to fly in atrocious weather conditions, had to pay a heavy price for their successes. In the first six weeks of their operations they lost on average three aircraft a week, mostly bombers, a very high proportion. Five bombers out of twenty were lost on a raid on Valona at the begin-

[38] WO 201/2727.

ning of December. However, although her contribution was relatively small, at least Britain was seen to be doing everything she could to help her gallant ally.[39]

The British Military Mission sent to Athens in November had as its first leader Major-General M. D. Gambier-Parry, who had been carefully briefed not to promise anything to the Greeks, or to enter into any commitments. He proudly reported to London on 5 November: 'I took the opportunity of asking Metaxas whether he had any ideas in mind as to the employment of British military forces making it clear that my question was on hypothetical basis that a force of which it was quite impossible to predict the strength or composition might be despatched at some future date.' He was at once rapped over the knuckles by the Chiefs of Staff. He must not discuss such matters, even hypothetically, lest it should raise false hopes. Undaunted, he telegraphed on 8 November: 'I may be wrong but recent straws seem to indicate that wind is blowing in direction of possible despatch of British military force to Greece. Hope I am not talking out of my turn when I urge most strongly that if this is so the commander designate and staff should be sent here earliest possible opportunity.' Gambier-Parry's hope was vain. This communication, coming so swiftly after his earlier indiscretion, must have caused a minor explosion in London. The Chiefs of Staff reply was explicit: 'You are entirely wrong in supposing that the wind is blowing in direction of possible despatch of British military force to Greek mainland and you are expressly forbidden by any word or suggestion of yours to imply such a course is contemplated. To raise false hopes would be disastrous.' Gambier-Parry replied contritely: 'Much regret misinterpretation of direction of wind and the resulting importunity.'[40] He did not have a third chance. Within days he was replaced by Major-General Heywood.

It was necessary to try to divine the intentions of the Germans in the Balkans. While it seemed likely by the

[39] CAB 66. Weekly résumés of the naval, military and air situation.
[40] WO 201/56, 24b, 55a, 70a, 74a.

middle of November that the Greeks would hold the Italians, if not throw them out of Albania, there was no doubt in the minds of the War Cabinet that if Germany joined forces with Italy it would be a very different story. Of the Balkan states only Yugoslavia and Bulgaria were now worth worrying about as possible allies. On 6 November, before the Italians had been halted, Metaxas asked Britain to press Bulgaria for an assurance that she would not invade Greece, so that he might safely move troops west from the Bulgarian frontier. Two days later, however, he got an undertaking from Turkey that she would guarantee the Bulgarian-Greek frontier, which enabled him to send substantial reinforcements to the Albanian theatre.

At this time the British government provided an assessment of the Balkan position for the benefit of Dominion Prime Ministers. It was confessed that the Italian objectives were not yet clear. Either they had made a premature attack on Greece, unco-ordinated with the Germans, to better their position vis-à-vis the senior partner; or, and this was considered to be the more likely, the move was part of a prearranged plan to divert British troops from North Africa. The Italian attack might be deliberately half-hearted simply to tempt the allies to send a force to Greece which would be suddenly pounced upon by a German descent through Bulgaria.[41]

On 22 November the War Cabinet still hoped that Bulgaria might be induced to take a stand favourable to the allies. She had been repeatedly warned by Britain against allowing herself to fall into the hands of the Germans; and she had been privately told by the Turks that they would go to war if she allowed the Germans to come in. The British Ambassador was instructed to ask the Turkish government to make this warning publicly so that no one would be in any doubt about their intentions, but they were not prepared to go so far. The War Cabinet discussed the case for trying to bring Turkey into the war

[41] FO 371/24916, ff. 111-13.

at this stage. The Chiefs of Staff thought that on balance it would help; but the Foreign Secretary disagreed on the ground that she would immediately ask for large quantities of arms which Britain could not supply. It was left simply that pressure would be brought to bear on Turkey and Yugoslavia to join in a common front; and that if they did so, Bulgaria would then be asked to form a tripartite alliance with them against German aggression.

Three days later the War Cabinet made a further assessment of the state of affairs in the Balkans. It seemed that Germany and Italy were both surprised by the strength of Greek resistance; and there was reason to believe that the Germans did not want the war in the Balkans to become general. If, however, they decided to intervene, it was probable that they would go through Bulgaria which would not put up a fight, rather than through Yugoslavia, which would. Churchill guessed that Mussolini had attacked Greece against Hitler's wishes, perhaps because he suspected that Germany had done a deal with France behind his back. If he was right, it might be that Hitler had no countermove ready to redress the balance; but it would be rash to draw a favourable conclusion. Germany might well be meditating a stroke on the lines most embarrassing to the allies, through Bulgaria to Salonika. Bulgaria might give her right of passage, and Turkey might be persuaded to stand aside. Not for the first time, events proved the Prime Minister to be right.

4. Hitler picks up the pieces: the Tripartite Pact

Mussolini's attack on Greece made it all the more necessary for Hitler to secure the loyalty of the uncommitted Balkan countries. His partner's manifest incompetence had raised doubts in their minds about the ability of the Axis powers to win the war, and if they were not brought into the Axis fold there was a real danger that they would side with the allies. There was, however, no problem with Hungary. The least she could do in return for favours received from the Vienna arbitration was to make a public declaration of her allegiance. This she did on 20 November 1940 by acceding to the Tripartite Pact between Germany, Italy and Japan, which had been signed on 27 September 1940.

Romania was next in line. Her Minister President, Antonescu, in spite of his pro-Nazi leanings, had the temerity to criticize the Vienna award while he was on a visit to Rome. A week later, on 22 November, he was severely reprimanded by an angry Ribbentrop who claimed that but for Hitler's intervention Romania would have been wiped from the map by Russia and Hungary. The Vienna award had been a reasonable compromise. Hungary had regained two-fifths of the territory lost after the first world war; and Romania had retained three-fifths of her gains. It might be difficult to stomach, but it had to be done. After much more in this vein Antonescu complained that Romania had been heavily punished for mistakes due to sinister forces, Bolshevists and Jews hiding behind the old régime. Nevertheless, she would now accede to the Tripartite Pact; and indeed go much further. She would shed her blood for the Axis on the field of battle.

Later in the day he met Hitler. It had no doubt been hoped that the preliminary canter with Ribbentrop would induce Antonescu to listen in humble silence to one of the lengthy expositions so dear to the Führer; but the Romanian insisted on repeating his earlier arguments, after summarizing Romania's history for the past two thousand years. For the first time ever she had been defeated without firing a shot, all because of the dark forces of Bolshevism. She faced economic crisis, and needed long-term credits at low interest rates. The stream of refugees from Bessarabia and Dobruja was endless. They had to be housed, fed and supported. He spoke bitterly about the treatment which the Romanian minority in Transylvania had received from the Hungarians. Many had had their eyes gouged, tongues cut out, fingernails torn off. However, in spite of her sense of grievance Romania would

join the Tripartite Pact and fight shoulder to shoulder
with the Axis powers for the victory of civilization.

Hitler was suitably sympathetic, but reminded Antonescu, as Ribbentrop had done, that conflict between
Romania and Hungary would have led to general catastrophe. Bolshevism would have eliminated the intellectuals
by murder or deportation to Siberia. He confirmed that
Germany wanted a prosperous Romania, and spoke of
commercial treaties under which Germany would buy
Romanian commodities at fixed prices for periods of ten
to twenty years. Finally, he referred to the invasion of
Greece by his ally, which had cast a momentary shadow
on the general picture. Italy had not paid sufficient heed
to geographical and seasonal factors; and her intervention
might encourage Britain to seek bases in Thrace. Germany
would oppose this with all her might; but she would
demand no military aid from Romania – merely the co-
operation of her General Staff.[42]

When Keitel said next day that the Germans wanted to
send another division to Romania Antonescu agreed provided that it would be self-supporting as regards both
finance and food. If his own people, who had just had a
very bad harvest, thought that they were feeding or financ-
ing German troops, it would lead to trouble. Keitel then
referred to the German forces which would have to be
launched south from Romania and Bulgaria, if the British
gained a foothold in Greece. Antonescu said that they
would present no difficulty so long as they were prepared
to make do with emergency barracks, for which he would
provide the timber. Later in the day Romania formally
acceded to the Tripartite Pact; and in a farewell audience,
on which Antonescu insisted, Hitler assured him that the
Romanian state would now have the full backing of the
entire Wehrmacht.[43]

Hungary and Romania were now secured. Bulgaria,
however, was unwilling to sell her soul without reservation.
Hitler invited Boris to join the Pact just before Mussolini

[42] *DGFP* xi, pp. 654-70.
[43] *Ibid.* pp. 684-9.

attacked Greece, but the King was unresponsive. He recited a gloomy survey of the probable consequences. So far his cautious policy had prevented the establishment of an anti-German bloc in the Balkans. To continue it would preserve the peace of the region – their common aim. The economic life of the Balkans would remain strong. On the other hand if Bulgaria joined the Pact her neighbours might consider themselves threatened, and strike before he could mobilize. His army, though brave enough, had only a handful of armoured vehicles, obsolete artillery, and a few days' supply of ammunition; and on his southern borders were twenty-three Turkish and seven Greek divisions on a full war footing. The old comradeship-in-arms between their two countries was as strong as ever – but was it absolutely necessary to upset Bulgaria's unequivocal and imperturbable policy, which had so far kept the enemy in check?[44]

Boris took the same line when he met Hitler at the Berghof on 18 November, after the Italian attack on Greece had begun. Bulgaria must not commit herself until the latest possible moment. This was amplified when the Bulgarian Minister (Draganov) had an interview with the Führer on 23 November. Bulgaria was quite willing to accede to the Tripartite Pact, but for a host of reasons the date must be deferred. For example, if the war materials she needed from Germany were delivered immediately after her accession it would excite suspicion in Russia – whose offer of assistance she had just declined – and in Turkey. The Balkan Pact of 1934 embracing Romania, Greece, Turkey and Yugoslavia, was still in force. The last three countries were still collaborating, which might present another threat. Hitler disagreed. The Turks were poorly prepared and would never attack. They knew that Constantinople would be wiped out in an instant just as Coventry and Birmingham had been. After Draganov had rehearsed other objections, Hitler conceded that Bulgaria must make up her own mind, but said he had no doubt

[44] *DGFP* xi, pp. 364-6.

that the right course was for her to join the Pact right away.[45]

Although Bulgaria was not at this time prepared to make a formal alliance with the Axis powers, she was quite happy to give Germany any facilities she needed within her borders. The German Legation in Sofia was instructed at the beginning of November 1940 to seek authority for the establishment of an air raid warning system along the Bulgarian-Greek frontier, which would mean sending 200 officers and men from Germany. This was because of the fear that the British would build air bases in Greece from which they could attack the Romanian oilfields; and the air raid warning system already set up along the Romanian-Bulgarian frontier might thus be bypassed. The Legation was warned that when they sought the approval of the Bulgarian authorities the proposal should be treated as a technical military matter without any political significance. Therefore it must be handled by the Air Attaché and not by the Minister himself. Every possible device must be employed to conceal the fact that the men installing the system were members of the Wehrmacht. Further, Bulgaria was to be told that she must see to it that no British planes flew over her territory unmolested.

The Bulgarian government's first reaction was to agree in principle to everything the Germans asked for; but they had second thoughts. They feared that if Luftwaffe communications troops were sent it could not be kept secret from British intelligence, and therefore asked that only a few instructors should be sent to work with Bulgarian technicians. The Germans, however, insisted that the necessary special units must come from Germany; but to meet the Bulgarians' difficulty they would wear civilian clothes. The new warning system was being set up at the end of November.[46]

Hitler now had the satisfaction of knowing that two of the Balkan states had formally pledged themselves to the

[45] *DGFP* xi, pp. 672-8.
[46] *Ibid.* pp. 479-80, 651-3, 672-8.

Axis. His margin of safety in south-eastern Europe had been considerably increased; and he had gone some way towards restoring the delicate balance which the Duce's deceit and stupidity had disturbed.

Although Hitler had said virtually nothing to Mussolini about his Greek adventure when they met in Florence on 28 October – it was only a few hours old and not even the Führer could tell how it would turn out – he was less restrained with Ciano on 18 November, and in a letter of 20 November to the Duce, when the adventure had become a fiasco. He said he had hoped to make his views known before the beginning of the threatening conflict with Greece, about which he had been informed only in a general way; and to suggest that the invasion should be postponed. In particular he would have proposed a lightning occupation of Crete before the Italian offensive started, assisted by German parachute and airborne troops.

The new situation had grave psychological repercussions which were prejudicing his diplomatic preparations for a grand coalition. Bulgaria was now completely opposed to joining the Tripartite Pact. Russia was showing an unwelcome interest in fishing in troubled waters in the Balkans. Yugoslavia's position was uncertain, and even in France the impression was growing that the last word in the war had not been spoken. The military consequences of Mussolini's precipitate action were no less serious. Britain was acquiring air bases which would bring her dangerously near the Romanian oilfields. 'I hardly dare think of the consequences; for Duce, one thing must be realized: there is no effective defence for oilfields.' He tried to make Mussolini's flesh creep by pointing out that the whole of Albania and southern Italy were now within easy reach of British bombers. It would be a matter of complete indifference to Britain if Italy destroyed Greek cities in reprisal raids.

He then announced his plans. There was now no question of *consulting* his ally. Spain must be prevailed upon to enter the war, so that Gibraltar could be seized. Russia must be enticed away from the Balkans and in-

duced to look to the east. There must be an understanding
with Turkey. Yugoslavia must be made to co-operate.
Hungary must allow the passage of German troops bound
for Romania. The Duce must reach Mersa Matruh to
establish an air base from which bombers could drive the
British fleet from Alexandria and mine the Suez Canal.
The Mediterranean question must be settled during the
coming winter. If the British established themselves in
Greece, German troops would advance against them
through Bulgaria. The last could not be done, however,
until the spring of 1941; and in any case Hitler must have
his troops back in Germany by the beginning of May at
the latest.[47]

Mussolini replied that he keenly regretted that his
letter of 19 October had not arrived in time to elicit
Hitler's opinion about invading Greece, which he would
have studied most carefully. The letter had been written
nine days before his offensive began – but he neglected to
add that its despatch had been carefully held up. He said
he was well aware of the repercussions, but he had no
doubt that they were passing phenomena. He was preparing thirty divisions to annihilate Greece, and was not
worried about the danger that his southern cities might
be bombed. He had no important industrial plants there.
The Italian people, goaded by failure, would give everything that was asked of them.

Hitler told Ciano that Yugoslavia should be bought off
with a guarantee of her territory and the promise of
Salonika when Greece was defeated. Ciano agreed, but
the final decision rested with the Duce, who could not
stand the Yugoslavs. Hitler dismissed this point by reply-
ing that he too had to cultivate relations with countries he
could not stand, perhaps having Italy in mind. Mussolini
in due course accepted without reservation that Yugoslavia's boundaries should be guaranteed, and her right
to Salonika recognized on condition that she acceded to
the Tripartite Pact; and no doubt as a gesture of appease-

[47] *DGFP* xi, pp. 607-8, 639-43.

ment he gave the Führer carte blanche to do whatever he thought necessary.[48]

The Yugoslav Foreign Minister was summoned to the Berghof on 28 November and assured by Hitler that there were no political differences between the Reich and Yugoslavia. The economies of the two countries were complementary. Germany had no territorial ambitions in the Balkans. Though by the spring of 1941 she would have at her disposal 230 divisions, and no foe of any consequence facing her, she was not aiming at imperial conquest; but for the sake of the balance of power in the peninsula she wanted a strong Yugoslavia. If Yugoslavia and Italy could come to an agreement Germany would ensure that Mussolini, whose blunder, nay criminal irresponsibility, in attacking Greece had weakened his position, would not tear it up when it suited his book. It would be terrible if the war had to be still further extended, but nevertheless Germany might have to intervene in Greece. Italy would then have to do as she was told about Yugoslavia. This had been made clear to Mussolini and he had accepted it. Hitler hoped that Yugoslavia would seize the chance thus provided. Germany would be attacking not the Greeks but the British, who would be thrown out as they had been thrown out everywhere else – even if it needed 180 divisions. He wanted nothing from Yugoslavia, not even the right of passage for troops, unlike the British. Ribbentrop added that Germany's policies in central Europe would bring about a golden age in which the nations could devote themselves to constructive progress.[49]

In spite of these blandishments Cincar-Markovic merely said he noted the points put to him. He would at once return to Belgrade to report to the Prince Regent.[50] In the event, however, many weeks were to elapse before the Yugoslav government was finally brought to toe the Axis line.

[48] *DGFP* xi, pp. 608-10, 639-43.
[49] *Ibid.* pp. 728-35.
[50] Halder, p. 206.

The Greeks had done everything humanly possible to maintain a position of technical neutrality. When they received the Italian ultimatum they hoped that the Germans might intercede on their behalf; but their Minister in Berlin was told by the State Secretary that the matter must be settled between Athens and Rome. Rizo-Rangabé called on Weizsäcker again on 4 November and spoke of the friendship which Germany had won in Greece over the last twenty years, which was now in jeopardy. He knew where the Germans' hearts really lay. Not so, said Weizsäcker, curtly. The Germans stood with their allies, the Italians.[51]

In fact, the Germans were not so much standing with their allies as bolstering them up. It was necessary to demonstrate to the outside world that the Reich still had every confidence in the Duce. Ribbentrop deemed it wise to send special briefing to the heads of all German diplomatic missions. They were to let it be known that the Italian offensive had been designed to seize a limited number of places which the British had been using as secret bases. The operation had been started with slender forces, and now had come to a standstill, mainly because of the season, but also because of the vastly superior numbers of the Greeks. The Italian retreat was a passing phenomenon (Mussolini's phrase) – a military incident of no importance in the long run. Further, it went without saying that German diplomats abroad must counter any criticism of Italy, and emphasize the solidarity of the Axis. In particular they must go out of their way to be friendly to Italians they met in the course of their duties.[52]

The Italian government was required to play its part in saving the situation. Ribbentrop said that the front must be stabilized on a line between Lake Ohridsko and Corfu. If this was held German propaganda could easily represent the Italian failure as an episode of no importance. Even if the line was broken, and the whole of Albania lost, it would have no bearing on the outcome of

[51] *DGFP* xi, p. 466.
[52] *Ibid.* p. 851.

the war; but it would mean a loss of Italian prestige difficult to repair. Therefore everything must be staked on holding the Lake Ohridsko-Corfu line.[53]

There was little more that Germany could do to pull Mussolini's chestnuts out of the fire – at least for the time being.

[53] *DGFP* xi, pp. 850-1.

III

1. Point of no return: Hitler looks east

On 3 September 1940 – the first anniversary of Britain's entry into the war – Hitler postponed from 15 to 21 September his proposed invasion of her south coast. A German navy memorandum dated 4 September, which had been in preparation for some time and must therefore be regarded as an independent professional assessment uninfluenced by knowledge of the Führer's decision to postpone Operation 'Sealion', set out the reasons why he would fail to break Britain and end the war in the autumn of 1940. The weather would be unsuitable. Neither the navy nor the Luftwaffe was strong enough to bring to a successful conclusion an attack on the British Isles. This realistic line may seem to be surprising, since there was still at this time a general presumption in Germany that Hitler must succeed in whatever he put his hand to, although it is true that the navy had always been doubtful about Sealion's chances of success.

Having written off Britain as a desirable objective, at least for the immediate future, the memorandum proceeded to examine other areas of importance to the British Empire which might be attacked. In practice this meant the Mediterranean region, since the rest of the Empire was considered for the moment to be beyond the reach of the Axis forces.

The most sensible course would be to attack Gibraltar through Spain; and to move through Libya to capture Egypt and gain control of the Suez Canal. This would enable the Axis to dominate the Mediterranean, with far-reaching benefits. The Rock could not be replaced by any of the Atlantic Islands – the Azores, Madeira, or the Canaries. When Spain entered the war on the side of the Axis, Portugal would be neutralized. Sea traffic round south-eastern Europe, in particular oil for Italy and Spain, could move unhindered. In the Atlantic the whole balance

73

of advantage would swing in favour of the Axis. Italian naval forces, working with the German fleet, could freely undertake tasks there. Italian land and air forces could support Germany in East Africa where the British colonies would be threatened. British power in the Indian Ocean would be vulnerable. The French colonies in North Africa would be prevented from going over to the British side. The raw materials of Arabia, Egypt and the Sudan would be readily available, and the attitude of the Balkan states assured. Turkey would give up all thought of taking arms against the Axis.

The domination of the Mediterranean was of supreme importance. Since the Italians could not handle the situation there with the requisite speed and thoroughness, German support and supervision would be needed. Therefore, as soon as the final decision about Sealion had been taken – whether to carry on with it, or to postpone it – the planning of operations in the Mediterranean area must be undertaken. There the war could be won.[1]

Admiral Raeder, Commander-in-Chief of the Navy, liked the recommendations, no doubt partly because of the major role which they assigned to the navy. He sent a copy to Hitler, who agreed in principle with what was proposed and ordered that further preparatory work should be carried out.[2] Raeder expounded his ideas to the Führer at a naval conference on 26 September when he asked permission to speak on matters outside his province. He said that the Mediterranean question must be settled during the winter. Gibraltar, the Canary Islands, and the Suez Canal must be taken with the help of German troops. It would then be necessary to advance from Suez through Palestine and Syria as far as Turkey. That done, 'it is doubtful whether an advance against Russia from the north will be necessary'. Hitler again agreed 'with the general trend of thought'. He considered that an advance through Syria would depend on the attitude of France, but it would be quite feasible.[3]

[1] MOD 578/131-3.   [2] MOD 578/129.
[3] *Führer conferences on naval affairs 1940*, pp. 104-6.

74

Mussolini's invasion of Greece just over a month later changed the whole strategic picture. On 4 November, again at a naval conference, Hitler described his ally's action as a regrettable blunder. On no occasion had he authorized him to do anything of the sort. (This, however, was questionable since the licence which he had given Mussolini in April 1940 'to improve his strategic position'[4] was arguably wide enough to allow the Duce to invade Greece with a clear conscience – except for his failure to keep the Germans informed.) It was self-evident that the Italians had begun their attack with wholly inadequate forces. Their stupidity had impelled Britain to occupy Crete and Lemnos and thereby strengthen her position in the eastern Mediterranean. The British were now well placed to move on to the mainland of Greece, to influence Turkey, and to bomb the Romanian oilfields. Fighters, fighter-bombers and anti-aircraft detachments must therefore be transferred to Romania immediately.

The possibility that German troops should be sent to the rescue of the Italians was then discussed. The plan would be to invade Greece through Romania and Bulgaria – with or without the latter's agreement – in the direction of Salonika and Larissa. It would take a month to make the necessary preparations. Bulgaria must be given military support as an insurance against a Turkish attack. It was expected that Russia would remain neutral, which would have some bearing on Turkey's attitude. The Führer, however, did not plan to take action against Turkey as a first step in breaking through to the Suez Canal from the east via Syria. He considered that this would be a very lengthy operation involving great difficulties.[5]

Hitler incorporated several of Raeder's ideas in his Directive No. 18 of 12 November 1940, which sketched out his plans for the immediate future. Spain would be brought into the war by political measures. Gibraltar would be captured and the Straits closed. Steps would be

[4] *Führer conferences on naval affairs 1940*, p. 23.
[5] *Ibid.* pp. 112-13.

taken to prevent Britain from gaining a foothold on the Iberian peninsula or in the Atlantic Islands. The employment of German forces in North Africa would be considered after the Italians had taken Mersa Matruh.

In the eastern Mediterranean, however, the action now contemplated was relatively limited – certainly nothing on the scale put forward by Raeder only a few days earlier, which Hitler had seemed disposed to accept. The army must be ready to occupy the Greek mainland, if it became necessary, but only to the north of the Aegean Sea, and not as part of a plan to gain absolute power in the whole of the Mediterranean. It was to be no more than a defensive measure to safeguard the right flank of his armies when in due course they invaded Russia, and to enable the Luftwaffe to attack any British air bases which threatened the Romanian oil fields. He would continue to control the Balkan peninsula by diplomacy rather than by force; but if diplomacy seemed likely to fail he would supplement it with the minimum amount of force needed to maintain stability. When Russia was at his mercy neither diplomacy nor the Wehrmacht would be required to bring the whole of the Balkans to heel. Then the domination of the Mediterranean, which would administer the *coup de grâce* to the British Empire, could easily be accomplished.

It must have been obvious to Raeder that Hitler had already made up his mind that Russia would be his next target, and that however strong the case for winning control of the Mediterranean there was no hope of making him see reason. But the navy was not easily defeated. Another memorandum – dated 14 November, two days after Directive No. 18 – restated much of what Raeder had been preaching, with modifications to take account of the spanner which Italy had thrown in the works by attacking Greece. Mussolini had greatly improved Britain's position in the eastern Mediterranean. He had enabled her to gain prestige in the Balkans, the Near East, Egypt and the United States. Equally, his strategic blunder had lost prestige for Italy. The occupation of Gibraltar and the control of the western Mediterranean, which Directive No. 18 legislated for did not go far enough. Control of the eastern Mediterranean was essential in both economic and strategic terms. It could be the key to victory. The Italians, who had no idea how damaging their offensive against Greece had been, had neither the military efficiency nor the leadership to carry out the necessary operations in the Mediterranean, from which the British must be thrown out. And in spite of the difficulties it was necessary that the Wehrmacht should mount an attack on Suez through Turkey.

All this was to no avail. Führer Directive No. 20, issued on 13 December, set out Hitler's intentions for the German invasion of Greece, and made it clear that he planned only a limited operation in the Balkans. It was intended to assemble German forces in southern Romania and to employ them via Bulgaria to take the northern coast of the Aegean Sea, and if necessary the whole Greek mainland. This at least was an advance on Directive No. 18. Because of the great political consequences the High Commands were to ensure meticulous direction in the military preparations. The offensive would begin when weather conditions were favourable – probably in March 1941 – and when the operation was successfully completed most of the troops would be withdrawn for use elsewhere. This of course meant that the defeat of Russia and not the domination of the Mediterranean was the Führer's next main objective.

Although the writing was now clearly on the wall, Raeder made a last despairing attempt to win the Führer over to his point of view at a naval conference on 27 December; but Hitler would agree only to those measures in south-eastern Europe which he conceived to be necessary for the success of Operation *Barbarossa*.[6] The Mediterranean grand design, the far-sighted blueprint for victory provided by the naval High Command, was not to be implemented.

[6] *Führer conferences on naval affairs 1940*, pp. 135-6.

2. Hoping against hope:
British policy January-February 1941

At the beginning of 1941 Churchill summed up the general war situation. So far as the Balkans were concerned the Greek resistance had been of enormous value. As soon as Tobruk was captured it would be expedient to provide more aircraft for the Greeks, who had been properly grateful for the small amount of help they had so far received. It might be possible to transfer four or five more squadrons from the Middle East, plus tanks and some artillery regiments. Further, they could include more modern aircraft, if the aerodromes could handle them. He was satisfied that support to Greece must have priority after the western flank of Egypt had been made secure. He saw it as the beginning of a chain reaction. If the Greeks could take Valona, the Italians would be driven out of Albania. Yugoslavia would be encouraged to cooperate. Thereafter Turkey might come in on the allied side. Wisely he added 'but we must not count on this'. The Defence Committee dutifully agreed. Two squadrons of Blenheim IVs and three of Hurricanes should be sent to Greece. They would have a better chance of taking on the Luftwaffe successfully than the Gladiators and earlier Blenheims already operating there. Tanks should also be sent.[7]

In the middle of January Wavell went to Athens from North Africa to tell the Greeks that Britain was prepared to increase her help as soon as Egypt was secured. He immediately ran into trouble. The Greeks did not want the sort of help that was offered other than aircraft, except that they were quite happy to accept captured Italian trucks, and clothing – in addition to the 180,000 pairs of boots and 350,000 pairs of socks already sent from North Africa. When Wavell told them they could have a combined anti-aircraft and anti-tank regiment, and a company of light tanks for the Albanian front they refused them politely, but quite definitely. Discussion about the defence

[7] CAB 69/2(2).

of Salonika was equally fruitless. Wavell pointed out that British troops could help the Greeks to offer strong resistance there, and at the same time demonstrate to Yugoslavia and Turkey that Britain was determined to support Greece to the utmost.

Metaxas could not agree. A small British expeditionary force would not ensure the safety of Salonika, but it would provoke a German attack. As a compromise he suggested that a British contingent which would be strong enough to take the offensive should land in due course in the Salonika region; but all preparations to receive it must be left to the Greeks so that before it arrived the British would not appear to be involved, and German retaliation would be deferred. After the Italians had been cleared from Albania large Greek forces would be available for the Salonika front, and then – but only then – would large-scale British help be welcome. Wavell argued as powerfully as he could in favour of the plan to send British troops right away, but it was useless.[8]

General Heywood, head of the British military mission in Athens, threw more light on the Greek attitude in a message to General Sir John Dill, Chief of the Imperial General Staff. It had become clear in the course of their meetings that Metaxas believed that Germany had no intention of intervening in Greece, and hoped that the attitude of non-provocation which he had adopted towards Italy in 1940 would succeed when applied to Germany. (It seems strange that he should have placed any reliance on the Italian precedent.) He wanted to play for time so that he could throw the Italians out of Albania, and then with Britain's help build a strategic reserve. He did not want to refuse British aid out of hand, but asked that it should be prepared and timed to achieve surprise without provocation.[9]

Churchill's reaction to the unforthcoming attitude of the Greeks was that they must be the judge of what should

[8] PREM 3/309/1, ff. 30-4.
[9] WO 201/100, 6A.

be done to help them. They must be made to realize that Britain was not trying to organize 'a Salonika front' but was merely seeking to support them with technical units. The Chiefs of Staff thought that the whole situation must be reviewed in the light of the Greek response to Wavell's offer – and also of the arrival of the Luftwaffe in the Mediterranean, which would alter the balance of power in the air; but if Britain made no move at this stage there was no chance of getting troops to Salonika before the Germans.

General Metaxas died on 29 January after a short illness, and was replaced as Minister President by Alexander Koryzis, a civilian and a much less strong character. Surprisingly he was less concerned about the danger of provoking the Germans to attack, perhaps because immediately he took office it became clear that the German infiltration of Bulgaria was reaching a climax.

British diplomats in the Balkan countries were doing what they could to counteract German pressure on Bulgaria; but they found it difficult to make bricks without straw. Indeed, some of their representations were counterproductive. Prince Paul of Yugoslavia, far from being comforted by the British proposal to send more military aid to Greece, professed that he found the idea alarming. He claimed that it would simply encourage the Germans to attack Salonika, and said he believed that if the British did nothing in the Balkans the Germans would not move further south.

It was of course of crucial importance that the British government should have accurate information about the German presence in Bulgaria. As soon as the enemy were well established there the case for sending reinforcements to Greece was weakened. It was equally important that the British view of the general situation should be clearly expressed to the Bulgarian government. The Legation in Sofia, the channel through which these objectives should have been achieved, was less successful than it might have been. Whether its failures made any difference in the long run is another matter.

In December 1940 the Foreign Office instructed the Minister (Mr G. W. Rendel) to give the Bulgarian government an assurance, which was intended to be a powerful warning. He was to tell them that their neutrality would be respected so long as it remained genuine, and was not impaired by the infiltration of German technicians, the conclusion of a military agreement with Germany, or adherence to the Tripartite Pact. Surprisingly Rendel decided off his own bat 'that the danger had passed' and took it upon himself not to pass on the warning. Equally surprisingly the Foreign Office, ever a generous master, decided to overlook his refusal.

On 10 January 1941, however, it was concluded that if a warning to Bulgaria was to do any good it must be issued right away. The Minister again tried to evade carrying out his instructions, again in the view of the Foreign Office without justification; but before his colleagues could weigh in with a reminder that British foreign policy was created in London and not at the whim of a Minister in the field, the Bulgarian Minister President publicly declared that his government would not submit to German domination. This declaration, which was in any case worthless, came after Rendel had failed for the second time to pass on the British government's warning, but the Foreign Office realized that he could now shelter behind it. They therefore simply instructed him to express appreciation of the position which the Bulgarians were ostensibly adopting. This episode suggests that at a critical period the British view was not put across to the Bulgarian government with the emphasis it deserved.[10]

Equally the information about the German forces in Bulgaria which the Legation fed back to London was woefully inadequate, and indeed misleading. For example, on 14 January Rendel telegraphed comfortingly that there was no German infiltration in Bulgaria on the scale experienced in Romania.[11] A week later he confirmed that German activities did not amount to occupation as in

[10] FO 371/29722, ff. 18, 27.
[11] *Ibid.* f. 81.

Romania, where several thousand 'instructors' had been allowed in. He believed, however, that their advance radio posts and technical experts had put the Germans into a position where they could start infiltration at short notice. If this happened 'we should soon hear of their being billeted and we should then be able to judge more accurately from their dispositions what Germany's immediate objective in this country is'.[12] President Roosevelt's special envoy to the Balkans, Colonel Donovan, took a more realistic view of the situation. He taxed the Bulgarian government with being unduly under German influence, citing for example the large numbers of Germans in the country, and recent Bulgarian legislation against the Jews.[13]

On 25 January Rendel reported a conversation with the Greek Minister who believed that the Germans had decided not to invade Bulgaria. His Greek colleague had suggested that the British Minister's 'recently repeated warnings' might have stiffened Bulgaria's attitude towards German penetration (the corollary of which was that his refusal to obey instructions might have weakened that attitude); but gave Donovan's visit as the more likely explanation. He had bluntly told the Bulgarians that Roosevelt and the American people were determined that Britain should win the war.[14]

The assessment of the diplomats, who should have been well placed to know the facts, contrasts strangely with an appraisal by the Joint Intelligence Committee made on 28 January – at which time the British Minister in Sofia was taking a relaxed view of the German threat. The Committee estimated that there had been a steady movement of German air force personnel into Bulgaria since the end of October 1940. There were now about 4,000 troops there, of whom between 500 and 600 were openly recognized as Luftwaffe. The German Air Attaché had a staff of 300. It was estimated that by the beginning of March –

[12] FO 371/29722, f. 92.
[13] *Ibid*. f. 108.
[14] *Ibid*. f. 95.

in just over four weeks' time – the German forces would
total about 10,000 men, which implied support for 400
aircraft. The preliminary occupation of Bulgaria could be
completed at short notice; but because of communications
difficulties it was reckoned that offensive operations based
on that country must wait until the beginning of March.
When Foreign Office officials saw this report they realized
that the situation was much more serious than they had
been led to believe by the Minister.[15]

On 2 February Rendel apparently awoke to the fact that
something was happening in his territory. He reported
that German troops were entering Dobruja and that
schools had been closed, possibly to provide accommoda-
tion for them. There was evidence to show that a German
military mission had arrived and that German infiltration
was proceeding at a faster rate. 'It is possible therefore,
though not yet certain, that Germans have already begun
establishing themselves militarily in this country and are
no longer waiting to begin a formal invasion until the
Danube is free of ice.' Next day, however, Rendel said
that the closure of the schools was *not* connected with the
arrival of any German troops, although in the meantime this piece of information had found its way into the
weekly resumé of the war situation prepared for the War
Cabinet.

The Minister also passed on an account of an interview
which his Service Attachés had had with the Minister of
War, who was as friendly as ever, and who promised to
send particulars of German technicians in Bulgaria.
Rendel thought that this information might be delayed,
and that when it *did* come it would not necessarily be
reliable – surely the understatement of the diplomatic
year. The Minister of War (who may have been amused
by the attention which the Attachés paid to his every
word) said he did not believe the Germans were proposing
to enter Bulgaria. The rumours that they were about to
move southwards were intended to divert Greek troops

[15] FO 371/29722, ff. 126, 131.

to the Bulgarian frontier and thereby relieve pressure on the Italians in Albania.[16]

Although the British government consistently took the view that the uncommitted countries in the Balkans were short-sightedly letting the allies down by remaining uncommitted there was a good deal of sense in the Turkish, Yugoslavian and Bulgarian positions, and in the half-committed Greek position. This is borne out by a strategical appreciation made by the British Foreign Office on the basis of their assessment of German aims. They guessed that Hitler might be contemplating the invasion of Greece through Bulgaria and possibly also through Yugoslavia, followed by an advance south eastwards towards the Bosphorus and the Dardanelles, with a view to operations in the Middle East. The Yugoslavs might resist, but Bulgaria could be bullied into giving German troops free passage. Turkey would then attack Bulgaria and the whole of the Balkans would be thrown into a turmoil.

The economic consequences for Hitler would be so serious that he would *not* move south at all unless he was forced to remove British troops from Greece. If the argument stopped at this point it confirmed that the Greeks were right in thinking that there was a good chance that they might be left in peace if they kept sizable British forces out of Greece; but the strategical appreciation went on to assume that Hitler had satisfied himself that a direct attack on Britain would not win the war for him, and that he would therefore turn his attention to the Mediterranean. This appraisal – which corresponds very closely to what was in Admiral Raeder's mind – led the War Cabinet to decide that Britain must put herself in a position to invade Greece as soon as the situation warranted it; and that the necessary preparations must be accelerated.

Churchill had never been in any doubt about the danger from Bulgaria. He told Wavell on 26 January that the Germans were preparing there for an action against

16 FO 371/29722, ff. 126, 132.

Greece, and urged him to lose no time in building up a strategic reserve which could be quickly moved to the Balkans.[17] In the War Cabinet a week later he pointed out that if German plans were allowed to develop unhindered south eastern Europe would witness in the spring a repetition of last year's events in Scandinavia and the Low Countries. Germany would bring Turkey to heel under the threat of bombing Istanbul and Adrianople. The only effective means of stiffening Turkish resistance was to send an RAF contingent to Turkey; but when this proposal was put to the Turks they had affected to regard the reports of German penetration in Bulgaria as exaggerated. They had also claimed that to accept the British offer would be tantamount to declaring war on Germany, for which they were not ready.[18]

The Defence Committee found it difficult to decide whether the Germans were bluffing in the Balkans in order to draw troops to that area, and thus facilitate the invasion of Britain; or whether they really planned a campaign in south eastern Europe, in the hopes that their attacks on shipping in the Atlantic, and on industrial plants in Britain would leave her an easy prey for later invasion. The Prime Minister could not accept that the Germans would limit themselves to defence in the Balkans; and in any case he thought it wrong to abandon the Greeks, who were fighting magnificently, so that the Turks, who were shirking their responsibilities, might be helped later. He believed that it would be possible to send four divisions to Greece, and another six to ten in the summer; and that there was a chance that the Germans would be held.

The main difficulty was that the Greeks had not declared their plan; and it was therefore impossible to determine how best to help them. It was agreed that the Chiefs of Staff should take as a working assumption that no serious operation would be undertaken in North Africa beyond Benghazi, and that when that town had been captured the largest possible force should be moved to

[17] PREM 3/309/1, f. 39.
[18] CAB 65/21, f. 17.

Greece. Certain special steps should be taken forthwith to concert plans with the Greeks. This cryptic sentence referred to the Prime Minister's decision to send the Foreign Secretary and the Chief of the Imperial General Staff to have talks with the Greek government, in the hope that they would make more progress than Wavell had done.

Although they were planning on the assumption that the worst would happen, the British government even at the eleventh hour strove to keep the Bulgarians neutral. Their Minister in London was seen in turn by the Permanent Under-Secretary at the Foreign Office (Sir Alexander Cadogan) on 14 February, by the Parliamentary Under-Secretary (Mr R. A. Butler) on 15 February, and by the Prime Minister – acting as Foreign Secretary – on 20 February, all of whom impressed on him the great mistake which his government would make if they threw in their lot with the Germans. Churchill said he well understood the difficult position in which smaller countries found themselves when threatened by a powerful and aggressive state; but even unsuccessful resistance would give Bulgaria a claim to sympathetic treatment in the peace settlement. Britain would win in the end, and she would certainly remember who her friends had been.[19]

3. Britain forestalled:
Operation Marita, January-February 1941

At the beginning of 1941 Hitler was like a charioteer driving a team of four ill-matched horses. Italy had learned her lesson the hard way in Greece, and was now docile and obedient. So also was Hungary, fed with the Vienna award. Romania still showed some signs of spirit, but on the whole was pulling her weight. Bulgaria, however, was not broken in fully; and Yugoslavia was not yet qualified for the team.

Hitler summed up the war situation on the eve of the New Year in a long letter to Mussolini. He began with a

[19] FO 371/29724, ff. 31, 37, 96.

comforting passage about Italy's failures in Greece and North Africa. Great powers often underestimated the strength of an enemy at the beginning of a war. German history had many examples. This sympathetic line highly delighted the Duce. Hitler then said he had been applying his mind to Italy's problems, and that satisfactory solutions would be found. In the Balkans, Romania and Hungary had taken a firm stand. He had no doubt that Antonescu realized that the survival of his régime – and his person – depended on a German victory. The Hungarians were no less determined and consistent; and in both countries everything possible was being done to facilitate the movement of German troops. Yugoslavia was watching and waiting, but had no intention of acceding to the Tripartite Pact. He thought there was no point in doing anything about this until further German military successes made her begin to see reason.

The Führer, resentful of Mussolini's deliberate failure to keep him informed about his Greek enterprise, would not reveal his plans at this stage, but told the Duce he might rest assured that Germany's future operations would be carried out with overwhelming force. Italy need do no more than consolidate the Albanian front and tie down the Greek forces there.[20]

Romania was still upset by the territorial losses she had suffered through the Vienna arbitration; and since she was to be used as a staging-post for a vast German army – more than 500,000 men would cross her frontiers – Hitler had to keep her well disposed. Antonescu told him in November 1940 that he was prepared to abide by the Vienna decision for the time being; but when peace was restored Romania would fight for her rights. Hitler replied that as a fanatical National Socialist he well understood the Minister President's aims. Antonescu, however, was very unsure of himself. When Fabricius was replaced as German Minister to Romania he imagined that it meant a change of German policy either towards his government,

[20] *DGFP* xi, pp. 990-4.

or himself, and was seriously worried. He was assured by the outgoing Minister that there was nothing to be alarmed about. The new Minister, Killinger, would carry on where he had left off. Neither German foreign policy, nor German interest in Romanian domestic affairs, would show any change.[21]

The first wave of troops to enter Romania was the so-called Wehrmacht mission, a reinforced armoured division. Then on 21 December General Erich Hansen, head of the mission, told Antonescu that it had become necessary to send a second division. He at once agreed, and fishing for information, hazarded the guess that the arrival of the new division might have something to do with an operation further south. Hansen made no comment. The Minister President then said that he had agreed to receive German troops to prevent the British from gaining a foothold in the Balkans. All that he asked was that they should be self-supporting, otherwise Romanians would go hungry. This point was taken and the German soldiers were reminded in orders that Romania was a friendly country. It was their duty to behave there as they would do at home. Further, they must take care not to buy things needed by the natives.[22]

Antonescu visited Hitler again on 14 January 1941, when the Romanian leader repeated his conviction that the British must be kept out of the Balkans. Hitler agreed. Britain would hand the peninsula over to Russia, but he would save it for Europe in the interests of all the individual states. The Führer also tried to reconcile Antonescu to his country's territorial losses, and he put in a word for the members of the Wehrmacht posted to Romania. They would be far from home, and they needed the goodwill of their host country. Moreover, it had been an achievement to get Hungary to allow the transit of German troops, and for the time being Romania must remain friends with her.[23]

[21] *DGFP* xi, pp. 662-70.
[22] T 78 329/6285537; *DGFP* xi, pp. 921-2.
[23] *Ibid.* pp. 1087-95.

The task of the forces assembled in southern Romania, which were to be commanded by Field Marshal List, was to push through friendly Bulgaria, keeping clear of Yugoslav and Turkish territory, towards the Aegean coast, and if necessary throwing the British out of Greece. General Hansen would announce right away that German units would be arriving in Romania, supposedly to protect the oil region. German engineers would establish themselves on the Romanian bank of the Danube to prepare for the construction of bridges.

There were at this time in Bulgaria a German reconnaissance staff of fifteen army officers and small navy and Luftwaffe groups in civilian clothing studying roads and operational conditions. It would be necessary to get the Bulgarians to carry out road improvements, for which German financial aid would be provided. The nearer the time came for throwing bridges across the Danube, which would depend on the weather, the clearer would become Germany's intention to move in with troops. This would create unrest in the Balkans, and probably alarm the Russians, to whom it would have to be pointed out that the troops were concentrating in southern Romania and therefore could not be directed against them, but were in fact to oppose the British whose presence in the region could not be tolerated.

Hitler had made it clear in November 1940 that Germany would have to occupy Bulgaria. King Boris was helpful. He explained that the roads in Bulgaria leading to Thrace and Macedonia would not be in a fit state to carry large numbers of troops until the beginning of March. He also begged Hitler to conceal his true intentions so that any unpleasant consequences would be deferred as long as possible. Although Hitler argued that if Bulgaria acceded to the Tripartite Pact it would help her to resist pressure from Russia, Boris was not yet prepared to take the plunge.

This presented the Germans with something of a problem. Bulgaria's co-operation was essential for the success of their designs on Greece, but the need for secrecy made them reluctant to give detailed information about their plans before it was absolutely necessary. When the Bulgarian Minister President visited Berlin at the beginning of January 1941 the Foreign Ministry's brief suggested that while there could be no question of discussing detailed military questions with him, it was necessary to prepare the way for the earliest possible staff talks about the passage of German troops, and Hitler's intention that the Bulgarian army should be used to cover the left flank of the German army and to keep Turkey at bay.[24]

Filov told Hitler that Bulgaria agreed in principle to join the Tripartite Pact, but still had misgivings about joining immediately. It was uncertain how Turkey and Russia would react, and the Bulgarian army was still inadequately equipped. Hitler replied that the sooner Bulgaria joined the sooner she would be out of all danger. If, as seemed likely, Germany was forced to take action against the British in Greece, precautions would have to be taken against Turkey. During their long conversation the two leaders made the same points over and over again. Filov was afraid of the consequences of joining the Pact. Hitler maintained that it was the safest thing to do.[25]

This had its effect. When Filov got back to Sofia he told the German Minister (Richthofen) that the Bulgarian government had virtually made up its mind to join the Tripartite Pact, although it still had misgivings about the military consequences. Nevertheless, talks between the German and Bulgarian General Staffs should start at once. The German Minister in Bulgaria reported to Berlin that his British opposite number had made a vain attempt to find out from Filov what the Führer had told him. Rendel had gone on to threaten that if Bulgaria joined the Axis Britain would bomb her cities to render them unusable by German troops, that the Turks would attack her, and that the Royal Navy would bombard Varna and Burgas from the Black Sea. When Filov suggested that the Russians

[24] T 78 329/6285553.
[25] *DGFP* xi, pp. 1018-27.

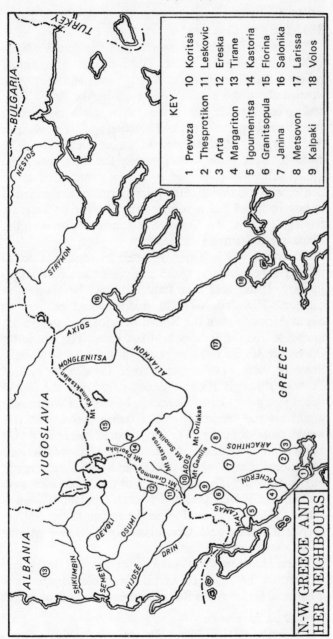

KEY

1 Preveza	10 Koritsa
2 Thesprotikon	11 Leskovic
3 Arta	12 Ereska
4 Margariton	13 Tirane
5 Igoumenitsa	14 Kastoria
6 Granitsopula	15 Florina
7 Janina	16 Salonika
8 Metsovon	17 Larissa
9 Kalpaki	18 Volos

N.-W. GREECE AND HER NEIGHBOURS

would hardly welcome the presence of the Royal Navy, Rendel had nothing more to say.

Richthofen admitted, however, that the British Minister's threat had some effect. The Bulgarian government believed that Turkey might attack them, and they were worried about the possibility of raids by the RAF. They had no anti-aircraft defences and even small-scale British attacks would provoke popular reaction against an alliance with Germany. But as soon as arrangements could be made to meet these contingencies, the Pact would be signed. This was confirmed by the Bulgarian Minister in Berlin, who was told that the price Germany was prepared to pay included her agreement that Bulgaria should be given an outlet to the Aegean Sea somewhere between the Maritsa and Struma estuaries.[26]

The plans which Hitler regretted he could not reveal to his partner were discussed at a conference on 8 and 9 January. Hitler said that Italy must not be allowed to collapse. Therefore German troops would be sent to North Africa to stem the British advance, and to Albania to ensure that the Italians held fast there. The troops for Operation *Marita* must be ready to move by 26 March. Some of them would be earmarked for defence against Turkey, although Hitler did not think that the Turks would take arms against Germany. Ideally, the Wehrmacht would assume command of the Italian forces, but this would cause difficulty. The Duce would resent it, and it might lead to demands for information about German operational plans – which the Italian Royal Family might leak to Britain.[27] The conclusions of this conference were embodied in Führer Directive No. 22. Operation *Sonnenblume* (Sunflower) would go to the rescue of the Italians in North Africa, and Operation *Alpenveilchen* (Alpine Violet) would go to Albania.

When Hitler met Mussolini at the Berghof on 19 and 20 January he indulged in his inevitable lengthy *tour d'horizon.* So far as the Balkans were concerned, he would

[26] *DGFP* xi, pp. 1080-81.
[27] *Führer conferences on naval affairs 1941*, pp. 8-13.

intervene immediately if the British landed in Greece. He would use in the Mediterranean the tactics employed against England – bombing the same target over and over again – and would thus compel the British to evacuate the whole region, taking the Royal Navy with them. He would leave nothing to chance in his march through Bulgaria – the question of transportation had been most carefully studied. It was essential to keep Yugoslavia quiet, and she had therefore been promised Salonika. Cincar-Markovic was an intelligent fellow who would not take any risks for the sake of Britain, but Prince Paul belonged to the international lodge of princes who put their dynastic interests first and foremost. Ribbentrop added that it was just as well that Bulgaria's accession to the Tripartite Pact should be deferred for a few weeks since it would be regarded by the British as a signal that the German army was about to march through Bulgaria. Next day Hitler harangued the Duce at great length on the military situation generally. He was now less positive about sweeping the British from the Mediterranean, conceding that it might be difficult to clear them out of bases in the Aegean Sea, and especially from Crete.[28]

Now that they had succeeded in pushing the Bulgarians to the brink, the Germans had no intention of allowing them to retreat. Richthofen was told by the Foreign Ministry in Berlin that it was assumed that there would be no more difficulty, but if the Bulgarian authorities suggested delay – for example, that the proposal to allow free passage should be considered by the Cabinet – they must be told that the die was cast. The decision of the Reich was unalterable, and the orders about troop movements had already been issued. If the Bulgarians hesitated the Minister was to point out the grave consequences that lay in store.

In the event it was unnecessary to issue an ultimatum. The Bulgarian Foreign Minister seemed to be relieved by the tough line taken by the Germans; and on 23 January

[28] *DGFP* xi, pp. 1127-33.

the Minister President formally agreed to sign the Tripartite Pact. There was no question of submitting the
decision to Cabinet. The Pact would be signed as soon as
conversations between the two General Staffs had been
concluded; and the promise of an outlet to the Aegean,
which had been given orally, was made more binding.[29]

All seemed now to be plain sailing for the Germans.
On 27 January the preparatory work on the bridges across
the Danube was in progress, and it was expected that they
would be ready from 10 February. The Luftwaffe and
anti-aircraft units would not enter Bulgaria until there
were bases there ready to receive them. Their movement
would need a hundred trains, and since the Bulgarian
railways could handle no more than six a day, sixteen
days would be needed. Anti-aircraft protection would be
provided for Sofia and Plovdiv, and also for Varna and
Burgas through which Bulgaria's oil was imported. It was
considered better on balance that the Bulgarian army
should not attempt a partially-camouflaged mobilization.
It could not be kept secret, and would lead to counter-
mobilization in Turkey and Yugoslavia. The Bulgarian
army, such as it was, would be used only to oppose a
possible attack by Turkey – although Ribbentrop believed
that the Turks might be best neutralized by means of a
non-aggression pact with Bulgaria. Jodl naturally hoped
to conceal Germany's objective as long as possible, even
when the Danube was being crossed. He proposed to pretend for a week or two that the German troops pouring
into Bulgaria were simply training units transferred at the
invitation of the Bulgarian government.[30]

Hitler ordered on 28 January that the entry into
Bulgaria must be delayed until the last possible moment.
It was too soon to say when the attack should take place,
but it could hardly be before 20 February. He agreed that
Bulgarian mobilization could not be concealed, and must
therefore await the arrival of the German troops; but the
Bulgarian air force, anti-aircraft defences, and civilian

[29] *DGFP* xi, pp. 1171-2.
[30] *Ibid.* 1210-12.

defences should be made ready in as camouflaged a form
as possible. He agreed that since it now seemed that
Bulgaria had come to heel – at long last – there was no
immediate need for her to accede publicly to the Tripartite
Pact. That could be done when the Wehrmacht arrived.
These decisions by the Führer were translated into a
Wehrmacht order by Keitel on 31 January.[31]

Two weeks later – on 14 February – Hitler issued his
final orders. The Bulgarians should now complete there
mobilization. The actual bridging of the Danube would
begin on 21 February, and at the same time the German
troops in Dobruja would enter Bulgaria. The Danube
would be crossed on 24 February. The Bulgarians must
be warned that 680,000 troops would be involved in the
operation, and they should be told that even this huge
number could be increased to deal with every conceivable
political or military development in the Balkans.[32]

The Bulgarians acquiesced in these proposals generally,
except that they asked that the bridging of the Danube
should be deferred to 28 February, and that the movement of troops into Bulgaria should start on 2 March. On
1 March Ribbentrop removed their final misgiving when
he confirmed in writing that when the new Balkan
frontiers were determined Bulgaria would receive her outlet to the Aegean. Ciano made a similar declaration. This
proposal was to be treated in the strictest secrecy, and
made public only if the Axis powers agreed.[33]

Also on 1 March Hitler wrote to the Turkish President
that Turkey was in no danger from Germany. German
troops in Bulgaria would keep well away from the Turkish
frontier. Germany's sole purpose was to stop the British
from gaining a foothold in the Balkans.[34]

While the Germans were making these massive preparations the Greeks were doing what they could to make
them unnecessary. At the beginning of December when the

[31] *DGFP* xi, pp. 1216-17, 1236-7.
[32] *Ibid.* xii, pp. 99-100.
[33] *Ibid.* p. 203.
[34] *Ibid.* pp. 201-3.

German Military Attaché in Athens (Hohenburg) asked the Greek Foreign Ministry about a report he had received from the Abwehr (the Wehrmacht's counter-intelligence service) that British land forces had arrived in Greece, he was given a categorical assurance that except for RAF units and their ground crews no British troops had landed in Greece, nor were any expected. Erbach added that he was satisfied that the Greeks were speaking the truth. He had earlier scotched a rumour that the British had asked to be allowed to attack the Romanian oilfields from bases in Greece. The Greek government had no wish to become involved in the Anglo-German war, and had asked for British help only for their defence against Italian aggression.

When Metaxas saw the German Minister at the end of December – an unusual event, for since the Italian invasion the Minister President had made it a rule not to receive heads of diplomatic missions – he assured him that there was no danger that a British military initiative would disturb relations between Greece and Germany. Despite her successes in Albania, Greece had no intention of making conquests, although she would of course need to have an assurance that she would no longer be exposed to a threat from Italy.

That Greece was doing her best to localize the conflict was confirmed next month by the Greek Military Attaché in Ankara. He told his opposite number in the German Embassy that there were no British troops in Greece, except in Crete, where there was only a base. British help for Greece had been limited to the supply of war material, and support from the Royal Navy and the RAF – and even that was nothing like the amount originally promised. Land forces had been refused since they could never be very effective, and would immediately call Germany into action. Greece's only aim was to secure herself against further Italian aggression.[35]

The anxiety of the Greeks to keep on the best possible

[35] *DGFP* xi, pp. 810, 916.

terms with the Germans is illustrated by an exchange between the Greek Minister in Berlin and the State Secretary at the beginning of January 1941. The Minister called on Weizsäcker to ask him to convey to the Führer a congratulatory New Year's message from the King. Weizsäcker had instructions to ask the Minister to return the Führer's thanks to the King. When Rizo-Rangabé got back to his office he realized that he was uncertain precisely what the State Secretary had said, and he telephoned him for confirmation. Had he asked him to convey the Führer's thanks, or his congratulations? Weizsäcker quickly made it clear that there was no question of congratulations, but only thanks.[36] On such niceties of protocol are the fates of nations balanced.

[36] *DGFP* xi, p. 1012.

IV

1. The fatal error: Eden in the Middle East

The capture of Benghazi on 7 February strengthened
Britain's position in North Africa and made it possible to
plan to send a much larger force to Greece – if the Greeks
wanted it. Churchill told Wavell on 12 February that the
Foreign Secretary and CIGS would come to Cairo 'to give
the very best chance to concerting all possible measures,
both diplomatic and military, against the Germans in the
Balkans'. The major effort for the immediate future must
be to help Greece, and possibly also Turkey. Both had
refused technical units because they thought they would
be too small to be of any use, but conspicuous enough to
provoke German intervention. However, that intervention
was becoming daily more certain and Britain's first
thought must be for her ally Greece. The Prime Minister
hoped to offer her at least four divisions from the army
which had defended Egypt – the implication being that
Egypt was now secure. If the Greeks had a good plan to
move troops from Albania to hold the fortified line near
the Bulgarian frontier, Britain should back it with all her
strength. He had no doubt that they *must* have such a
plan, since otherwise they would not have dared to pursue
their advantage in Albania regardless of the mortal danger
which a German attack through Bulgaria threatened to
their right flank and their rear.[1]

By this time it had become obvious that the Greeks
faced a critical situation in Albania. Their advance, so
spectacular in November and December 1940, had been
brought to a standstill by ever-increasing Italian reinforcements, which the combined efforts of the small Greek and
British air forces could not halt. The death of General
Metaxas on 29 January, and the knowledge that the
Germans threatened to invade, affected the morale of the

[1] Churchill, vol. iii, pp. 56-9.

army and of the nation as a whole. In reporting this General Heywood said that the belief was growing that without Metaxas the army could not go on winning. His successor, Koryzis, had neither his personality nor his pugnacious optimism.

Heywood, who was under instructions to discuss the sending of further British help, could make no headway. The King reaffirmed his determination to fight to the bitter end, but claimed that plans could not be made until the size of the proposed British force was known. This reveals the weakness of the Greek government's approach to a problem the solution of which was primarily for them. If they really meant to fight to the last, if necessary on their own, they should have made their dispositions accordingly. Their failure to grasp the nettle would make the British contribution too late. Heywood believed that the military and political situations would so deteriorate that the survival of the existing British force in Greece would be threatened.[2] He was told by Papagos that Greece would not ask for more British help until the Germans had actually crossed the Greek frontier. This singularly foolish proposition emanated from Koryzis, who was unaware that Metaxas had given a formal assurance that he would ask for British help as soon as the Germans crossed the Danube or the frontier of Dobruja. When the new President of the Council belatedly heard of this assurance he reaffirmed it, which was marginally better than waiting for the country to be overrun before calling in the British.[3]

Eden and Dill were delayed by bad flying weather and arrived in Cairo on 19 February. The Prime Minister told the War Cabinet next day that their mission was to examine what help could be given to the Greeks, and the prospects of inducing Yugoslavia and Turkey to come in on the side of the allies. If the Greeks opposed the Germans, Britain would have to help them to the full extent of her power. If, however, the Germans offered them attractive peace terms, they could not be blamed for

2 WO 201/100, 12A.
3 *Ibid.* 13A; PREM 3/309/1, ff. 56, 60.

accepting them, nor should that decision be taken too tragically. Britain would have done her duty and would have to be content with making her position secure on the Greek Islands. He hoped that it would not be necessary to put a large British force into Greece; and indeed it would be difficult to get a large force there before the Germans entered.[4]

The Foreign Secretary and the CIGS met the three British Commanders-in-Chief in Cairo on 21 February and quickly agreed that Greece must be helped. They believed that there was a good chance of halting the Germans in Greece; but it would be impossible at the same time to spare any help for Turkey. The force which it was proposed to send to Greece comprised an armoured brigade, the New Zealand Division, an Australian division, a second armoured brigade, and a second Australian division – to be sent in that order. Shipping would be difficult especially because of the danger of mines in the Suez Canal, but all accepted that Greece must have first call on any troops that could be spared. After he had reported this to the Prime Minister Eden received a telegram in which Churchill said: 'Do not consider yourselves obligated to a Greek enterprise, if in your hearts it will be only another Norwegian fiasco. If no good plan can be made, please say so. But of course you know how valuable success would be.'[5]

The key point to be settled with the Greeks, given that they were prepared to accept an allied expedition, was where would a stand be made against the Germans. Ideally the line would defend Salonika, but in the British view that was ruled out because of insufficient air power. A final decision would have to wait until the Foreign Secretary had concluded his discussions with the Greeks.[6]

On 22 and 23 February Eden, Dill and Wavell secretly met the King of the Hellenes, Koryzis and Papagos at the Royal Palace at Tatoi near Athens. The King assured

[4] CAB 65/21, f. 24.
[5] *Ibid.* 13, ff. 58-82; PREM 294/1, ff. 19-20.
[6] *Ibid.* 206/3, f. 173.

them, as he had already assured Heywood, that the Greeks would fight on no matter who attacked them, and whether or not they received help from outside. Indeed, according to Eden, he seemed almost resentful that anyone should be in doubt on the point. Koryzis handed over a written statement confirming that Greece would fight until final victory, and that she would welcome help from her allies. He was afraid, however, that inadequate help would merely precipitate German intervention.

It was at these meetings that the seeds of the failure of Operation *Lustre* – the allied expedition to Greece – were sown. Eden's first task was to get the Greeks to accept that they would defend the line of the Aliakmon river, a strong natural defensive position in the heart of Greece, where there was thought to be a good chance of stopping the enemy with the available forces. Wavell was satisfied that the only hope was to make certain of this line in as great strength as possible as soon as possible, in spite of the fact that the alternative line – from the mouth of the river Nestos to Beles – guarded Salonika and was shorter.

The significance of the two lines is clearly illustrated by a glance at a map of the Balkans. The most northerly part of Greece is a long relatively-narrow corridor running from west to east, bordered by the Aegean Sea to the south and by Yugoslavia and Bulgaria to the north. If the Germans attacked from Bulgaria they would have to fight their way along this corridor from east to west and could thus be met on a narrow front on the Nestos which roughly marks the western end of the corridor. But if they came through Yugoslavia they would enter northern Greece *behind* the Nestos line and fall upon the Greeks from the rear. The attitude of Yugoslavia was therefore considered to be crucial since it was presumed that a decision to defend the Nestos line must depend on her siding with the allies.

It was, however, not enough to know that Yugoslavia would try to resist the Germans. There must be reason to believe that she could hold them. With the fate of Poland

and the rest of Europe still fresh in their minds it is difficult to understand how Eden and his advisers could take Yugoslavia seriously into account. At best she could do no more than stage a brief delaying action – Churchill himself said as much in October 1940[7] – which would still allow the Germans to take the Nestos line from the rear. During the meeting with the Greeks on 22 February the British representatives 'made it clear that it would not be safe to count on Yugoslavia';[8] and in his memoirs Eden records that 'I emphasized that it was important that we and the Greeks should take our decisions independently of the attitude of Turkey and Yugoslavia, since if we waited to find out what they would do, it might be too late to organize an effective resistance to a German attack on Greece'.[9]

In spite of taking up this unexceptionable position, and in spite of the fact that Eden's military advisers were convinced that the only course was to go all out for agreement to man the Aliakmon line, the Foreign Secretary went on to say that there were three possibilities from the political aspect:

1) To withdraw the troops without waiting for Yugoslavia to declare herself.

2) To begin the withdrawal concurrently with an approach to the Yugoslav government.

3) To wait until Yugoslavia had made her intentions clear.

He confessed that there was not much hope of getting an early indication of the Yugoslav government's attitude, which was painfully true; but – and this is where he made his fatal mistake – he volunteered to send a Staff Officer to Belgrade to discuss the position with the Prince Regent.[10]

This ill-advised offer was accepted with alacrity by the

[7] See above, p. 51.
[8] PREM 3/294/1, f. 6.
[9] Eden, p. 200.
[10] PREM 3/294/1, ff. 27-9.

Greeks since it fell in happily with the temporizing line
which they had been following, and which it seemed they
had been on the point of abandoning. Anything that
would put off the evil day when they had to reveal to the
world that they had invited the British to send an expedition was to be grasped with both hands. The whole idea
of consulting Yugoslavia at the eleventh hour was a red
herring gratuitously introduced into the Tatoi talks at a
moment when the reluctant Greeks had been painstakingly
led to agree to fall back on the Aliakmon line. The
Foreign Secretary had played right into their hands and
given them an escape clause which in the long run proved
disastrous. It was later decided that it would be dangerous
to send a Staff Officer since Prince Paul 'might well find
himself unable to give a decision without referring to his
government, and not all of his Ministers could be trusted'.
It was agreed instead that Eden should telegraph to Paul
through the British Minister in Belgrade (Mr Ronald
Campbell) drawing attention to the danger to Salonika
which was inherent in German activities in the Balkans,
and asking for his views.[11] The Foreign Secretary then
returned to Cairo en route for discussions with the Turks
in Ankara.

For some time the Yugoslav government had been
running with the hare and hunting with the hounds. In
December 1940 they had proposed a non-aggression treaty
with Germany and Italy in response to the suggestion
that they should join the Tripartite Pact. A month later
the President of the Council assured the Greek Minister
in Yugoslavia that his country would resist if attacked by
the Germans, and would deny any request for the free
passage of German troops.[12] The British Minister was also
led to believe that Yugoslavia would modify her policies
in order to support the British line in the Balkans. Campbell's instructions were to speak to the Prince Regent on
the following lines: recent information reaching the
Foreign Secretary indicated the virtual certainty that the

[11] PREM 3/294/1, f. 31.
[12] WO 201/100.

Germans would advance through Yugoslavia on Salonika which was of course of vital importance to Yugoslavia. It had become urgently necessary for the determination of British policy to know with certainty what would be the attitude of Yugoslavia in the event of such an advance.[13]

Campbell had earlier suggested that King George VI should follow up a letter he had written to Paul in November 1940, to which the Prince Regent had replied two months later, saying 'I think you know that we won't allow any country's troops to march through this land without opposing them'; and Churchill agreed that the King should write again. The King's letter reminded Paul that his government had made it clear that they would resist an attack, and that the British government had shaped their policies in the Balkans on this understanding. They were now faced with vital decisions in the region, which depended largely on Yugoslavia as the central factor in south east Europe. The least Britain could expect from a friendly country was that Yugoslavia should now explain in confidence what her position would be.[14]

Churchill, anxious to leave no stone unturned, considered whether he too should make a personal approach to Paul, but decided that it was better to leave the Foreign Secretary to make the running.[15]

When Eden learned that the King was making a second appeal he told Campbell to hand over the two messages at the same time; and this he did on 24 February. The Prince Regent, no doubt feeling himself to be cornered, spoke at great length about his difficulties. The government was divided. It would be virtually impossible to resist the Germans. They could isolate the Yugoslav forces in the north, from which they dare not be withdrawn, as the Croats would then claim that they had been abandoned. Even if the forces in the north did withdraw there would be great problems over communications and supply in the mountains. Campbell reminded the Prince Regent

13 FO 371/30205, f. 173.
14 *Ibid.* ff. 162, 234.
15 *Ibid.* 30206, p. 8.

that the Serbs were eager for action against the Germans. It was, however, impossible to get any positive assurance from him. He would promise no more than that he would try to get a message to Eden in Ankara on 26 February.

On that date Campbell was summoned by the Assistant Minister for Foreign Affairs to be told that the Yugoslav Ambassador in Ankara had been instructed to hand over the government's reply to Eden. Surprisingly, he would give no hint as to what the reply was. The Foreign Office file notes that Prince Paul had a morbid fear of leakage, which might explain his reluctance to keep Campbell informed; but went on to say that it was more likely that the Yugoslav reply was unsatisfactory from the British point of view.[16]

This proved to be the case. The Yugoslav Ambassador, no doubt under instructions to hasten as slowly as possible, waited until the evening of 27 February before delivering his government's message to Eden. It simply said that in the existing circumstances Yugoslavia could not adopt a definite attitude, and begged that His Majesty's Government would not insist that she should try to. The Foreign Secretary can hardly have been surprised; but the essential point is that even if Paul had come down wholeheartedly on the allied side it would have made no difference to the final outcome.

2. The genesis of Lustre

Meanwhile the British War Cabinet were faced with the problem of deciding policy in the light of such information as they were receiving from Eden as he moved between Cairo, Athens, and Ankara. They met on 24 February to consider whether or not to open a new theatre of war in Greece. The Prime Minister said that both Eden and Wavell wanted to send troops to Greece. He thought that they had made out an impressive case, particularly since Wavell was a man who always wanted to be better than

[16] FO 371/30205, pp. 188-9, 192; WO 201/52, f. 15.

his word. His opinion carried particularly great weight since his first wish must be to finish off the North African campaign. Further, Dill had been cautious about the idea of going into Greece, since he was doubtful whether the Germans could be held on the mainland; but he too was now in favour.[17] (In fact, Dill had told the VCIGS that he had gone to the Middle East with the firm idea that forces sent to Greece would inevitably be lost, and that instead Turkey should be supported; but after hearing the Commanders-in-Chief on the spot he was satisfied that the only hope of saving the Balkans from being devoured piecemeal was to go to Greece with all the forces that could be spared as soon as it could be done.)[18]

The Chiefs of Staff had also recommended that an expedition be sent. They believed that substantial military advantages would be gained, though there was a risk of failure. The disadvantages of leaving Greece to her fate would be certain and far-reaching; but even the complete failure of an honourable attempt to help her need not be disastrous in the long run. At least it would make the Germans fight for what they wanted instead of getting it by default.[19]

The point was made in the course of the discussion that Colonel Donovan, who had been sent round the Balkan capitals by President Roosevelt, firmly believed that it was important to form a Balkan front. If Britain now forsook Greece it would have an adverse effect on opinion in the United States.

In summing up the Prime Minister said that if the Greeks were helped it might stiffen resistance in the Balkans as a whole. Greece, however, could be held or lost without affecting allied strategy in the widest sense. The outcome of the war depended rather on holding England (sic) and Egypt, retaining command of the sea, gaining command of the air, and keeping open the American arsenal. The operation would not be easy since

[17] CAB 65/21, ff. 26-7.
[18] PREM 3 206/3, f. 173.
[19] CAB 65/21, f. 27.

the troops would have to be supplied round the Cape; but
if the Greeks were going to fight the Germans, Britain
must fight and suffer with them. He had given instructions
for the necessary preparations to be put in hand, pending
the decision of the War Cabinet. If anyone had misgivings,
he must express them now.

With such a clear lead, it would have been difficult for
any member to disagree. All declared themselves in favour
of sending armed help to Greece, subject only to clearance
with the governments of Australia and New Zealand,
since most of the troops earmarked for the operation came
from those countries.[20]

The Australian Prime Minister (Mr Robert Menzies)
who was present agreed with the decision; but he was uneasy about the time it would take the force to get into a
defensive position. If the adventure was doomed to be a
forlorn hope it had better not be undertaken. Might he
tell his colleagues in Canberra that it had a substantial
chance of success? Churchill replied unhelpfully that the
Australian Cabinet must assess this in the light of the
advice they received from Menzies.[21]

Three days later Menzies told the War Cabinet that the
Australian government agreed with what was proposed;
but they were worried by the small size of the force, its
equipment, and the availability of ships for evacuation,
should that become necessary. The New Zealand government – consulted through the Dominions Office – also
thought the expedition too small, but agreed without
hesitation that their Division should be employed. They
added that it was 'a matter of great satisfaction to His
Majesty's Government in New Zealand that the Second
New Zealand Expeditionary Force should now be ready
to play the full operational role for which it was formed,
and moreover, that once again Australian and New
Zealand forces should be chosen to stand together in a
common theatre of war'.[22]

[20] CAB 65/21, f. 29.
[21] *Ibid.* ff. 27-30.
[22] *Ibid.* f. 38.

Churchill said he was deeply moved by these messages. Australia and New Zealand had responded magnificently to what was perhaps the most severe proposal ever put before Dominion governments. He had no doubt that the decision was right. It had been taken with full knowledge of the many difficulties. He asked the War Cabinet to put on record their high appreciation of the attitude of the two Dominions.[23]

The prospects of success for *Lustre*, as the expedition was christened, suddenly diminished on 1 March when the Germans openly occupied Bulgaria, the latest member of the Tripartite Pact. However, next day a highly optimistic assessment of the position in North Africa came in from Wavell. He claimed that the enemy in the desert must be short of transport. The distance from their base in Tripoli to Benghazi, now held by the allies, was 646 miles. There was only one road, and for more than 400 miles the water supply was inadequate. These factors limited the threat, and Wavell said he was satisfied that the enemy would not attempt to recapture Benghazi.[24]

On 4 March Churchill gave the War Cabinet a gloomy review of the worsening situation in the Balkans; but nevertheless, impressed by Wavell's optimism about North Africa, said that if he and Dill were still in favour of going into Greece he would not issue countermanding orders. The War Cabinet might, however, wish to take a final view of the whole position in the light of information coming in in the next few days.[25]

That information, in telegrams from Eden on 5 March, was disquieting. The Foreign Secretary had returned to Athens on 2 March for further talks, being under the impression that the movement of troops to the Aliakmon line had started immediately after his last visit. He was astonished to learn 'that the Greek government had failed to carry out the agreement reached on the 22nd February at Tatoi and that the order for the withdrawal of the

[23] CAB 65/21, ff. 32-3.
[24] CAB 65/22, f. 96.
[25] *Ibid.* f. 6.

troops from Macedonia had not yet been given'. The Greeks for their part said that it had been clearly understood that the manning of the Aliakmon line must await the Yugoslavs' reply to the Foreign Secretary. Whatever the merits of the claims of the two sides – they are discussed below[26] – crucial time had been lost, when time was of the essence.

In Eden's view the Greek operation would now be more hazardous than it had seemed a week ago, though he considered it by no means hopeless; but it was not only a question of time wasted. Papagos, without Metaxas to guide him, had lost confidence. He was now unaccommodating and defeatist. He considered that the German entry into Bulgaria meant that his withdrawing troops would be caught on the move. Secondly, to withdraw from Macedonia would cause panic among the civilian population and have political repercussions elsewhere. Thirdly, it was impossible to withdraw any troops from Albania since they were exhausted and greatly outnumbered. He therefore proposed to remain in Albania, and to hold the line of fortifications near the Bulgarian border, although he accepted that the Germans could not be held up for long. He suggested that the British troops should be sent piecemeal to Macedonia, although he thought it unlikely that they would arrive in time to be of any use.[27]

The subsequent discussions with the Greeks, which according to Eden at times 'painfully resembled the haggling of an oriental bazaar' produced three alternatives: to withdraw the offer of military support to Greece, which would be disastrous since it would eliminate Greece from the war, and have world-wide repercussions; to agree to Papagos's new plan to send the allied troops piecemeal to Macedonia; or to accept a much smaller offer of Greek troops for the Aliakmon line, and build up the allies' concentration there. In spite of his serious misgivings, and the fact that there was no authority from the Australian and New Zealand governments to use their troops in the

[26] See pp. 179-81.
[27] CAB 65/22, f. 17.

changed situation, Eden at last agreed with the Greeks to adopt the last course.[28]

Eden met the British Minister to Yugoslavia in Athens on 2 March to get a first-hand report on the situation in Belgrade; and as a result decided to make yet another appeal to Prince Paul. Campbell had suggested that the Prince Regent had already made up his mind to support the allies but was too fearful of the consequences of publicly committing himself. Eden therefore gave him a letter to carry to Paul in which he sympathized with his difficult position, but reminded him of Yugoslavia's probable fate if she succumbed to German pressure. The Minister was instructed to supplement the letter orally. There was good hope of holding a line in Greece; and the Yugoslav army, if it came in, would have the British alongside them.

When Campbell handed the letter to the Prince Regent on 5 March he 'showed considerable interest in our decision, and the fact that our effort would be a serious one'. He promised to give a considered reply the following day, but it was not until five days later that he summoned the Minister. He again made much of his difficulties. He was not free to decide as he would wish. He must ascertain the will of the people. If they wanted to join the Tripartite Pact he would not stand in their way. He had been advised that neither Yugoslavia nor Greece, even with Britain's help, could hold out against the Germans for more than a week. He had always been frank with the British government, and he would not now undertake to do something which might prove to be impossible.[29]

One of the results of Eden's second approach to the Prince Regent was that it gave the War Cabinet an excuse for not committing themselves irrevocably to Operation *Lustre*. Although it was accepted that the Yugoslavs' answer was likely to be unhelpful, it was agreed that the final decision to go ahead in Greece should await the result of the Foreign Secretary's letter. The expeditionary force

[28] CAB 65/22, f. 18.
[29] FO 371/30206, p. 21.

was not due to disembark until 8 March and until that date the position should be kept open, and no further commitments entered into. The Prime Minister told the War Cabinet that he had instructed the Foreign Secretary to conduct his negotiations with the Greeks on the basis that the despatch of troops was in hand, which should help to make the Turks and the Yugoslavs more co-operative; but he had left to him the decision to send troops, or to relieve the Greeks of their undertakings – which would of course leave them free to make terms with Germany.[30] It seems that at this point Churchill's feeling was that Operation *Lustre* would have to be called off.

In the small hours of 6 March a telegram went from him to Eden in Cairo agreeing that the situation had changed for the worse – so much so that the War Cabinet found it difficult to believe that Greece could be saved unless Turkey or Yugoslavia came in on the allied side, which now seemed most unlikely. Greece must not be urged into a hopeless resistance in which Britain could contribute little. Grave issues were raised by the proposed use of Australian and New Zealand troops, to which the Dominion governments might not agree in the changed circumstances. Churchill clearly had it in mind that Greece might have to be allowed to go without a fight; but he said that this would not be a major catastrophe so long as Turkey remained an honest neutral. On balance, it might be better not to intervene in the Balkans than to be ignominiously thrown out of Greece. 'I send you this to prepare your mind for what, in the absence of facts very different from those now before us, will probably be expressed in a Cabinet decision tomorrow.'[31]

When the War Cabinet met later in the day (6 March) it was agreed that their decision must await a reply to this telegram. Menzies was more worried than ever about using Dominion troops. When the earlier decision to send military aid had been taken, the operation, although con-

[30] CAB 65/22, ff. 8-12.
[31] *Ibid.* f. 18.

sidered to be hazardous, had offered a reasonable chance
of resisting the German advance. All the new factors,
however, were adverse; and in his opinion no reason had
been offered why the operation should now succeed. He
thought that the War Cabinet had not been well informed,
and that the action of the Foreign Secretary in committing Australian troops was embarrassing. He had had
difficulty in persuading his colleagues in Canberra to agree
to send Australians to Greece when it was first mooted;
and everything that had happened since told against the
expedition. The Prime Minister, however, said that the
agreement to send troops must stand, unless the Greeks
decided differently; but in any case there could be no
final decision until they heard again from the Foreign
Secretary.[32]

Eden's 'measured and deliberate reply'[33] (Churchill's
phrase) came on 7 March, and was laid before the War
Cabinet that day. He and the CIGS had re-examined the
position with the three Commanders-in-Chief. All agreed
that despite the grave risks the decision to go to Greece
was right. General Papagos's attitude had improved. He
was now helpful and anxious to co-operate.[34]

In acknowledging this telegram the Prime Minister
urged that preparations should go forward with all possible speed, adding that he was deeply impressed by the
steadfast attitude which Eden and his military advisers
had maintained. But, almost as if he was encouraging the
Foreign Secretary to change his mind, he said yet again
that the Greeks must not be urged against their better
judgement to fight a hopeless battle. 'It must not be said,
and on your showing it cannot be said that having so little
to give that we dragged them in by over persuasion. I take
it from your attitude . . . that you are sure on this point.'
By now Churchill knew well enough that the Greeks were
committed to fight to the bitter end, if necessary on their
own. The King had said so, and Koryzis had handed over

[32] CAB 65/22, ff. 23-7.
[33] *Ibid.* f. 53.
[34] *Ibid.* f. 46.

a memorandum saying so. It is conceivable that in his heart of hearts the Prime Minister thought that the operation should now be called off, and that he was testing whether Eden and his advisers wished to say so. However, if in the full knowledge of how little Britain could help, the Greeks were still resolved to fight to the death, then Britain must share their ordeal – not, be it noted, stand shoulder to shoulder until final victory.

Churchill went on to say: 'We must be able to tell the New Zealand and Australian governments faithfully that this hazard, from which they will not shrink, is undertaken not because of any commitment entered into by a British Cabinet Minister at Athens and signed by the CIGS, but because Dill, Wavell, and other Commanders-in-Chief are convinced that there is a reasonable fighting chance.' Finally, he told Eden that so far he had made no case for the operation other than *noblesse oblige*. A precise military appreciation was indispensable if the Australians and New Zealanders were to be convinced that *Lustre* should go ahead.[35]

If Churchill was trying to provide Eden with a loophole the Foreign Secretary did not take advantage of it. He said he had no doubt that all along the Greeks had been determined to fight, and welcomed British help. Secondly, he was convinced that there was a reasonable fighting chance, and that with luck the German plans might be upset. Dill and Wavell agreed with this.[36]

At this point there appeared on the scene a new adviser who may have finally convinced Churchill that the proposed expedition was a good risk even in the changed circumstances. General Smuts had been asked by Eden to come to Cairo to discuss the situation generally. Smuts told the Prime Minister on 7 March that he was satisfied that the Greeks must not be left in the lurch, although if the allies went into Greece the danger of a setback was very real. 'A firm British front in the Balkans would transform the situation in Southern Europe and the Mediter-

[35] CAB 65/22, f. 53.
[36] *Ibid.* f. 63.

ranean basin . . . I would thus urge most strongly that
this new front be supported with all our strength.' The
main need was for planes. He would bring another bomber
squadron from South Africa 'and Beaverbrook should
surely also disgorge from his hoard'.[37] The last suggestion
drew a sharp rejoinder from Churchill. 'Idea that Beaverbrook has a hoard of aeroplanes which he refuses to disgorge is pure nonsense.' Every possible aircraft had been
sent by every possible route, crated or flown to the Middle
East.[38]

The South African Prime Minister may have been confident that *Lustre* had a good chance of success, but his
Australian counterpart was not. Menzies was in the very
difficult position of having to look after Australian interests 12,000 miles from Canberra, without adequate
time for consulting his colleagues there. He told the War
Cabinet on 7 March that it was curious that the decision
to send troops to Greece was based on the trust which the
members reposed in the judgement of Eden, Dill, and
their advisers in the Middle East, yet all the arguments
which these men had advanced told against their advice.
This underlined the weakness of the position the War
Cabinet was taking up. The Prime Minister hastily replied
that a considered military appreciation, the conclusion of
which the War Cabinet already knew, was on the way
from Cairo. In his view it was their duty to go forward.
This silenced Menzies, and the War Cabinet formally
approved Operation *Lustre*. The Prime Minister would
telegraph the New Zealand and Australian governments
seeking their approval.[39]

Next day (8 March) Menzies sent a resumé of the
recent discussions to Fadden, the Acting Australian Prime
Minister. He explained that he had had a most anxious
time, but believed that he had put to the War Cabinet all
the points which had been troubling the Australian
government. The possibility of a successful thrust by the

[37] CAB 65/22, f. 60.
[38] PREM 3/206/3, f. 129.
[39] CAB 65/22, ff. 36-41.

Germans in North Africa had been discounted; and it was
believed that the Benghazi front could be held. But there
was no doubt that the plan to send troops to Greece was
not as good as it had been. Eden and Dill had made a
written agreement with the Greeks, and the consequences
of dishonouring it would be disastrous; and in spite of the
new and adverse circumstances Eden still thought that
there was a reasonable chance of success. Menzies said
that he had pointed out to the War Cabinet that Australia
would not refuse to take a risk in a good cause, but 'we
must inevitably feel some resentment at the notion that
a Minister not authorized by us should make an agreement binding upon us, which substantially modified a
proposal already accepted by us'. Churchill had taken this
criticism generously. Blamey and Freyberg – respectively
in command of the Australian and New Zealand forces –
agreed that the operation should go ahead; and a strong
cable had come in from Smuts, whose opinion he valued
highly, urging the formation of an allied front in Greece.
Menzies concluded by pointing out that the first troops
were already on the way, and asking for Canberra's early
agreement.[40]

In reply Fadden said that the Australian Cabinet
strongly deprecated the Foreign Secretary's action in
entering into an agreement about the use of Dominion
troops without prior consultation. They realized that Eden
had been in a difficult position, but nevertheless they felt
that if something like this happened again it might well
have 'far-reaching and unfortunate Imperial repercussions'. The Australian government's formal reply to the
War Cabinet was more restrained. They said that they
thought that Papagos's attitude as reported by Eden ('unaccommodating and defeatist') might reflect a substantial
body of opinion in Greece and indicate a lowering of
morale in the Greek forces. There was no doubt in their
minds that the Germans would go all out to inflict an
overwhelming defeat on any expeditionary force. Never-

[40] CAB 65/22, ff. 44, 65-8.

theless, 'the Commonwealth government steadfastly stands behind the British government in this high enterprise . . .'[41]

The New Zealand government's reply was received by the War Cabinet on 10 March. They considered that the operation, which they had always regarded as being highly dangerous and speculative, would now be much more hazardous. There was little prospect of help from Yugoslavia or Turkey, and the possibility of such help should be entirely discounted. There was a grave risk that the Greek army and the first British troops on the scene would be overwhelmed before the main British force arrived; and even when all the available British contingents were in Greece the position would continue to be extremely serious. The Germans had an almost unlimited number of divisions which could be poured through Albania, Yugoslavia, or Bulgaria, and efficiently reinforced from Italy. They would be moving on interior lines, whereas British reinforcements, their equipment and munitions could reach Greece only by a long voyage. The German and Italian air forces could easily be brought in great strength on troop concentrations, communications, transport and supply ships, and on the Suez Canal, which would be under constant attack. The RAF could make only a weak reply. The Italian fleet, and perhaps units of the German navy, would provide a serious threat to sea communications.[42]

From the opposite end of the earth the New Zealanders seem to have seen the dangers much more clearly than Eden, Dill, and the others who were in the Middle East; and events proved their assessment to be almost wholly correct. Logically, it should have led them to veto the use of their troops, which would inevitably have led to the cancellation of the whole operation; but in spite of their gloomy and realistic assessment they went on to say that they could not think of abandoning the Greeks to their fate, especially in view of their heroic resistance against the Italians. Therefore they fully agreed to the revised

[41] PREM 3/206/3, ff. 103-4.
[42] CAB 65/22, ff. 61-2.

proposal, and were confident that the troops themselves would be the first to applaud the decision. *Noblesse oblige* may not have been motive enough in Churchill's eyes but it was more than enough for those who controlled the destinies of the New Zealand Division – to their everlasting credit.

So *Lustre* was born out of a welter of uncertainty, inadequate consultation with the Dominions, doubt, and misgiving, and doomed to disaster by ill-advised reliance on the broken reed of Yugoslavia, and the muddle with the Greek government, which the British side should never have allowed to happen.

3. Prince Paul sits on the fence

Meanwhile the German preparations to occupy Greece were going ahead with all the ruthless certainty lacking from the allies' planning. On 1 March Hitler loftily told Ciano that the operation posed no great military problem. The only possible danger – one which had worried him all along – was that the British might bomb the Romanian oilfields. He guessed that as soon as he attacked, the Greeks would withdraw from the corridor between Bulgaria and the Aegean Sea. He thought that they might attempt some resistance at the western end of the corridor which was a mere fifty kilometres wide, and made up of swamps and mountains with only two good roads; but whatever the resistance, it would be quickly brushed aside.[43]

Hitler's confidence that the invasion of Greece would go without a hitch must have been increased by reports from the German Ambassador in Turkey, who said that Eden's visit to Ankara had achieved nothing and passed on the Turkish Foreign Minister's view that the British would not send a sizable force to Greece. Bulgaria's accession to the Tripartite Pact had not worried the Turks at all. This was confirmed by the Naval Attaché, who

[43] *DGFP* xii, pp. 206-10.

believed that the Turks would remain neutral in the face of a German occupation of Bulgaria, unless they were provoked by Germany, or there was massive pressure from Russia that Turkey should enter the war – which he thought unlikely. The occupation of the Greek coast and the Aegean Islands might upset Turkey, but she would not resist it. The Attaché reckoned that the Greeks would not oppose a German invasion so long as it was understood that the Italians would not be allowed to set foot on Greek territory.[44]

The Führer's letter telling the Turkish President that his objective in occupying Bulgaria was to enable him to throw the British out of Greece, and not to threaten Turkey was delayed in transit and was handed over by the Ambassador only on 4 March – by which time Eden had left Ankara. The President was grateful for the assurance that German troops would be kept at a safe distance from the Turkish border; and he told the Ambassador that Turkey would do everything in her power to avoid war with Germany. He purported, however, to be deeply concerned about Bulgaria's mobilization, which it seemed could be directed only against Turkey. Papen hastened to tell him that this was not so.[45]

But it was Yugoslavia, not Turkey, that was to dominate the scene in the next few weeks. She was the centre of a tug-of-war in which Germany always had the stronger pull, although Britain strove to draw her into the allied camp. The fundamental question was would she accede to the Tripartite Pact, following the example of Hungary and Romania; this was anything but an easy question for the Yugoslav government. The component parts of Yugoslavia – Serbs, Croats, and Slovenes – had not yet had time to coalesce into a unified state; and since the Serbs were anti-German and the Croats and Slovenes pro-German, the government found itself in an almost impossible position. Whatever they did must be wrong in the eyes of a large part of the community.

[44] MOD 90/889; 91/7.
[45] *DGFP* xii, pp. 201-3, 216-17.

The Yugoslav Minister President (Cvetkovic) and Foreign Minister met Ribbentrop at Fuschl on 14 February. Later on the same day they met Hitler at the Berghof, when Ribbentrop was again present. In the first meeting Cvetkovic said that Yugoslavia had striven to maintain peace in the Balkans. She had done, and would continue to do everything possible to supply Germany with the food and raw materials she needed. He believed that Britain was endangering peace in the Balkans, and that Yugoslavia could play a useful role in creating a bloc to exclude her from the peninsula. Ribbentrop agreed, and referred to Hitler's well-known desire for friendship with Britain. The Führer had been badly let down by that country, which in opting for war had committed the greatest folly in her history, as Churchill must now admit in his heart of hearts. He was, however, a skilful propagandist, and saw Britain's catastrophic defeat at Dunkirk as a glorious retreat, and magnified the capture of a few strips of desert into a resounding victory. There was no doubt that Germany would win the war. She was going from strength to strength, while Britain was losing on all sides. Now was the moment for Yugoslavia to take a clear stand by acceding to the Tripartite Pact. Cvetkovic said that he still hoped that peace could be established in the Balkans through diplomacy. If he was wrong there would still be time for Yugoslavia to join the Tripartite Pact.

In the afternoon Hitler echoed much of what Ribbentrop had said. Germany had not wanted the war. She bore no responsibility for its origin, or for its extension to the Balkans. The villain of the piece was Churchill, who had been agitating for war since 1936. Germany was not involved in the Italo-Greek war, and therefore could not take a position on the Yugoslav proposal to end it by a diplomatic initiative. This was purely and simply a matter for Italy. For his part Cvetkovic assured the Führer that he was doing his best to prevent the British from gaining a foothold in the Balkans. He still hoped that Yugoslavia's plan to achieve peace there by diplomatic means would

[46] *DGFP* xii, pp. 79-96.

succeed; but if it failed, she would still be free to align herself with the Axis.[46]

A week later the Yugoslav Minister in London (Soubbotic) called on Mr R. A. Butler, Parliamentary Secretary at the Foreign Office, to tell him about these meetings. They had been courteous, and the Germans had made every attempt to be friendly. Their line had been that Yugoslavia must quickly make up her mind to become part of the new order in Europe, and so on. In his record of their talk Butler noted that Soubbotic observed rather archly that the Minister President's meeting with Hitler could be compared with the Munich period of British policy, to which he gave a sharp but appropriate reply. Unfortunately Butler did not spell out precisely what was appropriate in this context. The British Minister in Belgrade made his contribution to the information available to the War Cabinet. He had been told by the Yugoslav Foreign Minister that they had received *no* invitation to join the Tripartite Pact.[47]

Cvetkovic had asked that Hitler should receive Prince Paul at an early date, and the two heads of state met at the Berghof on 4 March. The Führer said yet again – and at great length – that Britain had lost the war, and that the collapse of Greece was imminent. If only Yugoslavia would join the Tripartite Pact her future was assured. Prince Paul was visibly impressed but claimed that he was faced with a very difficult decision. He was quite open with Hitler and explained that the things that counted against accession were the fact that his wife was Greek, his personal sympathies for Britain, and Italy's hostile attitude towards Yugoslavia. He suggested, however, that it might be possible to negotiate a separate agreement with Italy, rather than to aim at full membership of the Tripartite Pact, with all its attendant obligations. Hitler at once seized on this and said that Yugoslavia need do no more than accede to the Pact. She would not have to go to war; and when peace was restored she would be re-

[47] FO 371/30243, ff. 7, 18.

warded with Salonika. The Prince Regent replied that having regard to domestic politics in his country he feared that if he followed Hitler's advice he would not be around in six months' time. Ribbentrop, who was also present, said that he would not be around if he *didn't*. At the end of the meeting Paul said that he wished to reserve his decision.[48]

There was no doubt that the Yugoslav government was in a very difficult position, from which they could escape only by being allowed to have their cake and eat it. When they discussed the question of accession to the Tripartite Pact shortly after Paul's meeting with Hitler they asked that certain points should be clarified. If Yugoslavia acceded would she be given a written declaration that her sovereignty and territorial integrity would be respected? Further, would it be agreed that German troops would be given no right of passage through Yugoslavia, and that she would not have to provide military assistance to the Axis? Finally, would the Germans put in writing their promise that the case for providing Yugoslavia with an outlet to the Aegean would have favourable consideration when Europe was reorganized after the war?

Ribbentrop dealt with these points on 9 March. Germany would certainly guarantee Yugoslavia's sovereignty and territorial integrity; and she would also give an assurance that no military aid would be called for from Yugoslavia, so far as the Greek war was concerned. Nor would there be any difficulty about ensuring that justice was done in due course about giving her access to the Aegean. But that was as far as he could go. Yugoslavia, like all the other signatories to the Tripartite Pact, might be required to provide troops for purposes other than the Greek war. In practice, military aid would probably not be called for, but it must be accepted that in the last resort it *might* be necessary.[49]

On 10 March the British Minister had a long talk with the Prince Regent who took much the same line with him

[48] *DGFP* xii, pp. 230-2.
[49] *Ibid.* pp. 255-6.

as he had done with Hitler. His wife was Greek, he was not free to do as he would like, and so on: but he left the impression that he would really prefer to side with the allies.

On the same day Cincar-Markovic said that Yugoslavia was perfectly well aware of the military obligations imposed on members of the Tripartite Pact, and that she could not possibly accept them. If she did it would lead to serious trouble since her people would conclude that she was being led into war with Russia or the United States. Heeren pointed out the stupidity of joining the Pact, and then seeking to opt out of one of its main provisions; and he rubbed in that while neither Germany nor Italy wanted to involve Yugoslavia in war, there could be no exception in her favour.[50]

The Germans, however, were so anxious to get Yugoslavia into the Axis camp that Ribbentrop agreed that the military obligation in the Pact should be watered down so as to be almost meaningless. He provided a new formula. If at any time Yugoslavia considered it to be in her own interest to participate in military operations as required by the Tripartite Pact, it would be left to her to make the necessary arrangements with the other signatories. This understanding would not be made public. Cincar-Markovic agreed, but asked that if it became necessary 'for compelling domestic reasons' he should be allowed to publish the understanding. That is to say, if there was trouble among that sector of the population who believed that accession to the Tripartite Pact would involve Yugoslavia in a major war, the government could then reveal that this was not so.

This brought Ribbentrop to the end of his tether. The Reich had been so accommodating that it was quite unreasonable for Yugoslavia to ask for anything more. The Foreign Minister went on to set out Germany's final position. Yugoslavia's territorial integrity and sovereignty would be guaranteed, and this could be made public on

[50] *DGFP* xii, pp. 257-8.

the day she acceded. That German troops would seek no passage through her territory could also be announced – in a form to be agreed with Germany – and Yugoslavia would not be required to come into the war against Greece. Finally, and this was a remarkable concession, he agreed that she would not be called on to provide military assistance elsewhere; but in no circumstances could this be made public since the other signatories would obviously take it amiss, and the whole basis of the Pact would be shaken. In any case it would still be necessary to get the agreement of Italy and Japan, the other founder members of the Pact. Cincar-Markovic said he would seek the early acceptance of this formula by the Crown Council. The British Minister in Belgrade, whose ear was nearer to the ground than that of his colleague in Sofia, was able to pass the substance of this to London on 22 March.[51]

The real difficulty of the Prince Regent's position now became apparent. When the German proposals were put to the Crown Council three Ministers, representing important elements in the Serbian population, resigned in protest. It would take time to replace them, and it seemed that Yugoslavia's decision about joining the Pact must be deferred indefinitely. This was not good enough for Ribbentrop. He said it was necessary in Yugoslavia's own interest to speed things up, and he gave 25 March as a deadline. The Japanese Foreign Minister was due in Berlin on 26 March and after that date negotiations with the Yugoslav government would have to be set on one side. He urged Heeren to do everything possible to persuade them to sign.[52] Campbell's assessment was that while it was obvious that the Crown Council was trying its hardest to put off a decision they could not delay it much longer. The only hope was that popular feeling in Serbia might reach such a pitch that the government would be forced to resign. On the evening of 23 March he was summoned by the Prince Regent to be told that the Germans had now imposed a deadline after which the

---

[51] FO 371/30206, p. 42; *DGFP* xii, pp. 291-4.
[52] *Ibid.* pp. 335-6.

special terms which they had offered would be withdrawn. He – the Prince Regent – still maintained that Yugoslavia would fight to the last; but Campbell concluded that she was now lost. The sudden imposition of a time limit by the Germans had done the trick.[53]

The threat of a deadline was in fact enough to pull Paul off the fence on to the Axis side. On 25 March the Yugoslav Minister President went to Vienna with authority to sign the Pact. Hitler, much relieved that his blandishments of the preceding weeks had borne fruit, was in an expansive mood. He had always been a sincere friend of Yugoslavia – if she ever got into trouble she would find him a loyal mediator, broker and friend. He knew how difficult it had been for Prince Paul to make the decision to join the Pact; but when Yugoslavia won her outlet to the Aegean those who disliked the decision would see it as the most successful act in the history of Yugoslavian foreign policy. Cvetkovic replied that his country was ready to co-operate with the new Europe, which must bring better justice to all the nations than the old had done; and she would certainly take advantage, in case of need, of the Führer's offer of future help. Later in the day Hitler met Ciano and indulged in self-congratulation at Yugoslavia's accession. He regarded it as being of great importance for the military action against Greece since the main railway line through Bulgaria, which would have to be used by German troops, ran dangerously near the Yugoslav border for nearly 400 kilometres.[54]

The Counsellor at the German Legation in Belgrade (Gerhard Feine) reported to Berlin that the announcement of Yugoslavia's accession to the Tripartite Pact had caused surprise. The government had made no attempt to prepare the people for this change of policy; and for the time being few were aware of the great opportunities which lay ahead. The government had taken all the necessary measures to suppress demonstrations, and was entirely in command of the situation. Feine spoke too soon,

[53] FO 371/30206, pp. 42, 44.
[54] *DGFP* xii, pp. 354-61.

however, and his Minister had to follow up his report next
day with the news that the pro-German government had
been thrown out. The young King Peter had broadcast a
proclamation that he had ascended the throne and replaced Cvetkovic with General Dusan Simovic. Hitler's
diplomatic triumph had been short-lived. Diplomacy must
now be replaced with armed force.[55]

At a conference on 27 March when Göring and Keitel
were present the Führer said that it was just as well that
Yugoslavia had appeared in her true colours before
Operation *Barbarossa* was under way. Even so, that
operation would have to be postponed for four weeks.
Yugoslavia must now be smashed. She would get no
ultimatum, but would be attacked as soon as the troops
were ready. It was essential that this should be done with
lightning speed and the greatest severity. This would
prevent the Turks from interfering, and it would have its
effect on the course of the Greek campaign. The Croats
would side with the invading Germans, and would have
to be told that in due course they would be rewarded with
autonomy. Operation *Marita* must start as soon as possible
with the objective of capturing Thrace and the Salonika
basin, and the high ground in the neighbourhood of
Edessa. This would be accomplished by a thrust through
Yugoslavia; a second attack from south of Sofia towards
Skoplje to relieve pressure on the Italians in Albania; and
a third from Sofia towards Belgrade. The Italians would
have to suspend operations against Greece to cover the
Yugoslav border and protect the German right flank.[56]

While Hitler was thus setting in motion a merciless
attack on Yugoslavia that country's new Foreign Minister
(Momcilo Nincic) was seeking to persuade the German
Minister in Belgrade that his government would continue
to co-operate with the Axis powers, although he confessed
that he was uncertain what position they would take on
membership of the Tripartite Pact. Heeren left him in no
doubt about the consequences of a change of policy to-

[55] *DGFP* xii, pp. 364, 368.
[56] *Ibid.* pp. 372-83.

wards the Axis. His advice to Berlin was that the Yugoslavs would remain friendly, but return to a policy of
neutrality. Since the new government was assured of
strong support from the Serbs they might be able to
sustain an unpopular foreign policy, although the Serbian
members of the Crown Council did not like the Tripartite
Pact.[57] Hitler's patience, however, was at an end. He was
not prepared to wait and see how the new government
shaped up. Führer Directive No. 25 of 27 March laid
down that even if the Yugoslavs declared their loyalty to
the Axis they must be regarded as enemies and destroyed
as quickly as possible. On the following day Simovic
assured Heeren that the *coup d'état* which had brought
him to power was simply the result of domestic politics.
He had always been a friend of Germany's, and was proud
of his acquaintanceship with Göring, to whom he sent his
regards. He would ensure that the situation was quickly
got under control.[58]

Three days later – on 30 March – the new Foreign
Minister continued the government's efforts to remain on
friendly terms with Germany. He assured Heeren that
they would respect international treaties concluded by
their predecessors, including accession to the Tripartite
Pact. The German Minister said that he could do no more
than note this statement, but he did ask how it could be
reconciled with the views of the Minister President as
expressed to the Italian Minister, which suggested a less
friendly policy towards Germany. Nincic was visibly disturbed by this, and said that Simovic must have been
speaking personally and not on behalf of the government.
On the same day Heeren was recalled to Berlin, and
instructed that in his absence only junior members of the
Legation should have dealings with the Yugoslav government. Earlier Ribbentrop had ordered him not to attend
any official function, if necessary giving illness as the
reason, and not to send anyone to represent him. A representative was to be sent, however, if the government sum-

[57] *DGFP* xii, pp. 383-4.
[58] *Ibid*. pp. 421-2.

moned the Minister to receive an official communication at a time when he was supposed to be out of action because of illness.[59]

On 2 April Feine reported that morale generally was low. People were having second thoughts about the *coup d'état*, and it seemed likely that the government would be willing to make concessions in order to avoid war. The Minister of Transport (Jeftic) believed that Yugoslavia could guarantee to follow domestic and foreign policies satisfactory to Germany including adherence to the Tripartite Pact. It was mooted that two of the new Yugoslav Ministers would go to Rome to call on Mussolini to mediate on their behalf. It was too late, however, for the government to save themselves from Hitler's wrath. Feine was ordered to reduce the size of the Legation to four or five men. All secret files must be destroyed as soon as the code words 'Tripartite Pact' were received. Feine was to let it be known to friendly Legations in Belgrade that these steps were being taken so that they could draw their own conclusions.

Next day Nincic asked to meet Feine, but he was told that this was not possible, although he could speak with a junior member of the Legation. He refused to do this, and instead saw the local representative of the *Deutsches Nachrichtenbüro*, the German news agency. He told him that the Italians had invited him to go to Rome to discuss the situation, but he believed that it was preferable to negotiate directly with Berlin. He was ready to go there at any time. The agency representative said that the Foreign Minister 'gave the impression of being practically prostrate'. The desperate position of the new government was confirmed on 5 April when the Foreign Minister's brother presented himself at the German Legation and said that it was hoped that direct conversations between Yugoslavia and Germany might begin that evening. He turned up again an hour and a half later and said that the entire government agreed that the Foreign Minister

[59] *DGFP* xii, pp. 412, 422-3.

should go to Berlin. He entirely supported the Tripartite Pact, and although Yugoslavia had received many suggestions from abroad he would listen only to the proposals he might receive in Berlin.[60]

Back in Berlin Heeren prepared a memorandum for Ribbentrop in which he pleaded for a moderate policy against Yugoslavia. Punitive action against Belgrade would be felt to be unjust even in Yugoslav circles well disposed towards Germany. Any action regarded as unjust and brutal could have an undesirable effect on the Croats; and if any Croatian Minister was harmed the political consequences might be very grave. It was widely recognized in Yugoslavia that Germany must clarify the situation quickly and completely; but there would be a serious loss of prestige for Germany if enemy propaganda was allowed to question the chivalry of German warfare. In the event Heeren agreed not to present this paper to Ribbentrop, perhaps because it was too near the bone, but instead said what he had to say orally. However, the die was cast, and nothing that he or anybody else could say would make Hitler change his mind.[61]

[60] *DGFP* xii, pp. 431, 436-7.
[61] *Ibid.* pp. 444-6.

V

1. Italian failure: January-March 1941

In December 1940 Mussolini dismissed Marshal Badoglio, Chief of the General Staff, and replaced him with Ugo Cavallero, who took over the command of the forces in Albania. Badoglio was no more responsible for the failure of the Italian invasion than any of his colleagues – or Mussolini himself – but a scapegoat had to be found. Cavallero flew at once to Albania, where he found a sorry state of affairs. Organization was chaotic. Casualties, for which there was nothing to show but panic retreat, had been very heavy. The winter was even more severe than usual, and many of the troops were suffering from frost-bite. Not infrequently men had frozen to death. Although Cavallero was nominally in command, he was subjected to a bombardment of instructions from Mussolini, who was becoming desperate, and seemed to believe that the more violently he exhorted his commanders the more likely they were to achieve the victory which would restore his prestige. His anxiety to make some progress against the Greeks was heightened by the knowledge that the Germans were planning a humiliating rescue operation. If his armies did not accomplish something soon, he would be the laughing-stock of the world.

Shortly after Cavallero arrived in Albania the Duce wrote him a letter, the tone of which confirms that he believed that he had only to ask for the impossible and it would be achieved. Cavallero was ordered to call before him his senior commanders and tell them that a successful attack was essential so that the situation, particularly from the point of view of morale, might be transformed. For two months Italy had been the anvil. Now she must become the hammer. The pending offensive must be carried through with great elan, and must leave the world in no doubt about the military standing of Italy. Germany had offered a division to lend a hand in Albania, but this offer must be rendered pointless by an Italian victory. Mussolini concluded by telling Cavallero to order his divisional commanders to go to the front and to remain there until the operation was completed. There must be no question of trying to direct the battle from a safe distance.[1] The last instruction shows that one of the reasons for the Italians' earlier failure was well understood; but it was one thing to issue an order like this and another for it to be obeyed.

In spite of the Duce's exhortations, it was the Greeks who were to take the initiative. They too were suffering from the rigorous conditions, but at least they knew that they had right on their side. They launched an attack in the centre of their line on 30 December and made some progress in the direction of Klissoura, but their lines of communication, through most difficult country, had lengthened with their advance, whereas the enemy lines had shortened. The Italians had been able to bring in large reinforcements, and to strengthen their air force. Both sides continued to mount small attacks designed to improve their local positions, but broadly speaking the two armies continued to face each other along the line from Pogradec and Lake Ohridsko in the north to Tepelene and the Adriatic coast a few miles north of Corfu which had been stabilized in December 1940. It was not until 9 March that the Italian spring offensive was launched.

The British contribution continued to be only in the air and even this was restricted by poor weather conditions. Nevertheless by the middle of January the RAF had destroyed forty-three enemy aircraft for the loss of twenty-three of their own.[2] Strategic bombing raids were carried out against the Albanian ports and key points behind the Italian lines. In February, however, the Greek High Command again begged D'Albiac to provide close support for their troops, whose morale – no less than the Italians' – needed to be boosted; and this time he gave way, with

[1] Quoted by Cervi, pp. 199-200.
[2] CAB 65 (weekly resumés of naval, military and air situation).

great reluctance, although he had to admit, at least to himself, that the number of aircraft at his disposal was so small that even if they had continued to concentrate on the ports of disembarkation it would hardly have affected the final outcome. Further, right from the beginning the RAF had been handicapped by the Greeks' anxiety not to precipitate a German invasion. They had been denied the use of aerodromes in the Salonika region, and even the right to make studies of them for future use. This meant that they had to fly greater distances than was necessary whether they were engaged in strategic bombing missions, or providing support for the ground forces.[3]

This question of provocation weighed very heavily with Metaxas. At the end of December heavy rains took their toll of the aerodromes in northern Greece and left Salonika as the only point from which the northern Albanian ports could be attacked. On 30 December Metaxas agreed with the greatest possible reluctance that the RAF should establish a bomber squadron there, but the very next day he changed his mind. The squadron must not move to Salonika until his government had had a chance to consider the possible effect on the Germans. They might see the move as a threat to the Romanian oilfields, and launch an immediate attack on Greece. Nothing must be done to provoke Germany until Italy had been dealt with, and Turkey and Yugoslavia were surer. As a concession the Minister President agreed that an RAF officer should be allowed to reconnoitre the airstrips at Lemnos and Mitylene. Even at the beginning of 1941 the Greeks were still refusing permission to use the Salonika aerodromes, although by this time the German threat was plain for everyone to see.

In spite of his belief that strategic bombing was to be preferred, D'Albiac recorded that the use of aircraft to support the troops was in the event successful – at least 'from a purely local and spectacular point of view'.[4] His newly-arrived Hurricanes made their first sortie on 20

[3] *Supplement to the London Gazette*, 7 January 1947.
[4] *Ibid.* p. 209.

February, and in an engagement a week later destroyed twenty-seven enemy aircraft without a single loss to themselves.

Mussolini decided to visit Albania in the hope that his presence would raise the morale of the troops on the eve of the spring offensive. He flew there on 2 March, manifestly apprehensive about the reception he would get from the men whom his crass stupidity had condemned to months of hardship and unnecessary suffering. As it turned out his fears proved to be groundless. The troops, perhaps gratified that the Duce was prepared to submit himself to even a tiny fraction of the danger and discomfort which they were enduring, gave him an enthusiastic reception wherever he appeared. Early on the morning of 9 March he stationed himself on a vantage point overlooking the Desnizza valley where he could view the main offensive from a safe distance.

Originally two plans had been put forward. The first, which made good strategic sense, was that the Italians should attack from the region of Pogradec at the eastern end of their line. Their invading forces would become one claw of a pincer movement, the other being provided by the Germans entering Greece further east. If successful, this combined attack would surround a great part of the Greek forces, but the plan was hardly likely to commend itself to Mussolini. The final rout of the Greeks must belong to him and to him alone. Therefore the alternative plan, which was advocated by Cavallero, won the day. This was that as many troops as might be necessary to achieve victory would be thrown against the Greeks in the sector between the Aoos and the Osumi rivers, much in the style of the more senseless attacks of the first world war. It was believed that sheer weight of numbers must win the day.

The Italian High Command hoped to induce the Greeks to transfer troops from the intended point of attack by laying on exceptionally heavy barrages in other parts of the front; but this deception – the only attempt to introduce subtlety into the plan of campaign – did not succeed. The Greeks' intelligence services left them in no doubt where the attack would come, and they were well prepared for it. It was an utter failure. Day after day huge infantry forces, involving twelve specially-prepared divisions, were hurled against the strong Greek positions; and day after day they were thrown back with disastrous losses. At first every assault was hailed in signals from the front as a breakthrough, but Mussolini, to whom victory meant everything, was not taken in. He quickly realized, before his generals would admit it, that they had failed again. Another fiasco was in the making.

The attack was called off on 16 March, although for ten days more there was sporadic activity along the front. The Italians had lost 12,000 dead and wounded, and had not gained an inch. Mussolini returned to Italy on 21 March. There was nothing for it now but to wait for the German rescue operation, whatever the cost to his pride.[5]

2. Ray of hope: The Yugoslav coup

Operation *Lustre's* chance of success was presumed by the British government to depend to some extent on the position of Yugoslavia; and now for a brief moment it seemed that their hopes about winning over that country had been fulfilled. The right-minded element in the Yugoslav population had rejected the German alliance. King Peter had called on all his subjects – Serbs, Croats, and Slovenes alike – to rally round him. It was their only chance to save the country. The British Minister in Belgrade, however, believed that the new régime would follow a policy of strict neutrality, although they might take a stronger line against German designs in the Balkans. Since their predecessors had not ratified the Tripartite Pact it was possible that the new government would regard it as a dead letter.[6]

[5] For detailed accounts of the Italian spring offensive see Papagos, pp. 300-7, and Cervi, Ch. 2.
[6] FO 371/30207, p. 8.

Churchill was elated. He had thrown all his weight into the campaign to bring Yugoslavia into the allied fold. On 22 March he had sent a personal message to Cvetkovic telling him that Hitler and Mussolini faced certain defeat. If Yugoslavia stooped to the fate of Romania, or committed the crime of Bulgaria and became accomplice in the attempted assassination of Greece, her ruin would be certain and irreparable. Four days later he instructed Campbell:

> Do not let any gap grow up between you and Prince Paul or Ministers. Continue to pester, nag, and bite. Demand audiences. Don't take NO for an answer. Cling on to them, pointing out Germans are already taking the subjugation of the country for granted . . .[7]

The news that King Peter had taken over the government seemed to confirm that Britain had won a substantial diplomatic victory. Without waiting to meet the War Cabinet the Prime Minister made the most of the new development. He asked Eden and Dill, who were in Malta on their way home from the Middle East, to return at once to Cairo to concert events. He authorized Campbell to inform the new régime that Britain recognized them as the government of Yugoslavia subject to their denouncing the Tripartite Pact, and helping in the defence of Greece. He sent a message to the Turkish President saying that affairs in Yugoslavia appeared to offer the best opportunity of preventing German domination of the Balkans; and to President Roosevelt urging him to use his influence to support the elements in the peninsula which were determined to resist German penetration. Finally, he ordered that the RAF units in Greece should be strengthened. All this the War Cabinet later noted with approval.

Churchill was also quick to point out to the Australian government that in spite of their earlier misgivings about Operation *Lustre* its chances of success were now improved. A month ago the operation had seemed a rather bleak adventure dictated by *noblesse oblige*, but the events

[7] Churchill, vol. iii, p. 142.

in Belgrade had shown the far-reaching effects of the action Britain had taken in the Balkans. German plans had been upset, and it was reasonable to hope that a Balkan front of 70 allied divisions might be formed – although this was by no means certain. But *Lustre* was now placed in its true setting not as an isolated military act, but as a prime mover in a large design. Whatever the outcome, everything that had happened since the decision to commit troops in Greece showed that the operation was justified. It would now be possible to organize a full concentration of the allied forces in Greece instead of throwing them in piecemeal. The Prime Minister confessed that the final outcome was still unpredictable, but the prize had increased and the risks lessened.[8]

The Foreign Office also left no stone unturned in their efforts to take advantage of the new situation. It was even mooted that King Peter should be provided with a British military adviser. Happily this idea was not put to the new government, which had come to power as a result of a *coup d'état* of the Serbian element in the army, which would hardly welcome the sudden appointment of a British officer over their heads. Campbell, still under Churchill's instructions to pester nag and bite, believed that the Legation Chaplain, who was an intimate friend of the Yugoslav Royal Family, could do his bit to exert influence on King Peter. Simovic, the new Minister President, was even induced to agree to meet Eden, in spite of the presumed danger that such a meeting would accelerate a German invasion.

It soon emerged, however, that all this was pious and unprofitable scraping of the barrel, mere clutching at a sheaf of diplomatic straws. There was no real foundation for the allies' new optimism. On 28 March Campbell reported that although there was no doubt that the situation had changed in Britain's favour, the question of the Tripartite Pact – the key to the whole situation – was still under discussion, and there was no certainty that it would

[8] PREM 3/206/3, ff. 82-3.

be denounced. Then the Minister President changed his mind about receiving Eden because of his fear that it would provoke the Germans. The new régime believed that sooner or later they would receive an ultimatum from Hitler, but they wanted to put off the evil day as long as possible, ostensibly to give them time to consolidate their domestic situation, since the Croats had not yet confirmed their support of the new régime. In reality Simovic and his colleagues, whatever they may have suggested to the British Minister, were hoping that the Germans would respect their neutrality. Had it been possible for the Minister President to receive Eden in Belgrade in complete secrecy he might conceivably have agreed to a meeting, but he was certain that the news of any meeting was bound to leak. To this Eden suggested that they could meet in his aircraft at a military airfield, but Simovic still refused.[9]

Dill at least was allowed to visit Belgrade for talks with the Yugoslav General Staff and the Minister President, but he could not make any progress with them. The new government was no less divided than the old, and seemed just as much to have their heads in the sand, hoping as other Balkan governments had done that time would prove to be on their side. On 4 April Churchill appealed to Simovic saying he could not understand his argument about playing for time. The German army and air force were concentrating for an attack on Yugoslavia, and what was wanted was a decisive forestalling thrust by the Yugoslavs into Albania.

It was too late, however. Hitler stuck to his decision that Yugoslavia should be given no ultimatum; and at 5.30 am on 6 April he announced that the invasion – Operation *Punishment* – had begun. Just over an hour later the first waves of German bombers began a merciless assault on the defenceless capital, which was to be carried on almost non-stop for three days. The Yugoslavs now made a pathetic appeal for help from the RAF but nothing

[9] FO 371/30207, pp. 83, 123-4.

could be done to help them. Their indecision had to be paid for.

3. Lustre meets Marita

The terms of reference of the German forces destined for the Balkan campaign were defined in orders issued at the end of December 1940. They were to use Romania and Bulgaria simply as assembly areas and were not to regard them as operational zones. They were, however, to make a distinction between the two countries. Romania was already a member of the Tripartite Pact, and presumed to be friendly. Therefore the Wehrmacht's powers vis-à-vis the civilian authorities there would be no greater than they would be in Germany. The use of postal services, the railways, the requisition of billets and food and so on would be arranged in accordance with agreements to be made with the government. The same general line was laid down for as yet uncommitted Bulgaria, but if relations with the Bulgarian government broke down, then the Wehrmacht was empowered to proclaim laws and penalties, and to issue orders to the Bulgarian civilian and military authorities. By the time *Marita* was under way, however, Bulgaria too was a member of the Tripartite Pact, and so far as the Germans were concerned in the same formal position as Romania.

Greece was of course to be deemed an operational zone, and it was taken for granted that there would be no difficulty in subjugating the country, which would then be administered in accordance with the army commander's full military powers. His first task was to ensure the maintenance of law and order and the speedy restoration of the economy. The army would conduct itself in such a way that the running of the country could be taken over by civil affairs units at the earliest moment. The rank and file must maintain correct relations with the civilian population and exercise restraint in all their dealings with them. Thus, whereas *Lustre* was planning to withdraw almost before it had reached its forward positions, *Marita* was planning with supreme confidence for the administration of occupied Greece.[10]

The only real difficulty which the Germans foresaw was how to handle the Italians. They were under no illusion about their value as allies and realized that it might be disastrous if they were treated as equal partners. It was nevertheless necessary to pay lip service to the idea of equal partnership since the Italian contribution to the Axis effort was better than nothing, provided that it was properly controlled; but the Duce's *amour propre* must not be upset by a too high and mighty line. Notes prepared for a discussion with Hitler about the arrangements for the occupation of Greece recorded that the part to be played by Italy would depend on the political concessions that Germany was prepared to make. It was accepted that the Wehrmacht would have to break down Greek resistance; but at least the mopping-up operations could safely be entrusted to the Italians. The Wehrmacht was ordered to support the Italians in Albania with officers of the Luftwaffe and the navy. The Mediterranean area was the responsibility of the Italians, and during *Marita* there must be close co-operation with the Italian navy since certain specific tasks would be assigned to it during the occupation. This must be discussed between Berlin and Rome at the highest level since the Italian General Staff had too little authority to deal on matters of this nature. Experience had shown that it was unwise to insist on offensive operations by the Italian fleet because of its weakness; and although it would be given responsibilities in the Mediterranean area the ultimate control would have to remain with the German Admiral Commanding, Balkans. The keynote of the Germans' policy was to keep the Italians in their place without appearing to do so.[11]

It was with this in mind that Hitler on 5 April wrote a hasty letter to Mussolini to keep him in the picture. He explained that it had become essential to use force in the Balkans since he had failed to win over Yugoslavia by

10 T 78 329/6285604-7.
11 MOD 50/823; 90/100-2, 923, 950; 578/162.

diplomacy. He had reluctantly decided, especially in view of the landing of British troops in Greece, that a military settlement was now necessary. Further, he believed that Russia was about to conclude a pact with Yugoslavia, so that there was not a moment to waste. His attack would begin next day.

He then went on to define Italy's role. The front in Albania must be held at all costs. In particular, any attack from Yugoslavia must be repulsed. The Wehrmacht and the Italian forces must act as a team, and he therefore proposed to inform Mussolini personally of his recommendations or wishes, which the Duce as Supreme Commander of the Italian Armed Forces would then issue as his own orders. This arrangement would be kept secret so that there would be no need for anyone to know that Italy was taking orders from Germany. Mussolini summoned the German Ambassador at 2 am on the morning of 6 April and said he was in full agreement with the Führer's proposals. He considered that it was the only conceivable solution of the command situation. For good measure the Duce spoke with enthusiasm about the brilliant planning of Operation *Marita*, which he had no doubt would destroy the enemy with the speed and precision of the Wehrmacht's earlier campaigns in Europe.

Two hours later the code words 'Tripartite Pact' were signalled by Ribbentrop to the Legation in Belgrade. The Chargé d'Affaires was to act in accordance with his earlier instructions. Secret material must be destroyed. Radio equipment was to be hidden 'under the coal pile or the like'. The staff of the Legation were to leave the city limits of Belgrade to find sanctuary at some suitable place of their own choosing – and they must ensure as far as possible that their movements were kept secret. This left Feine and his colleagues only an hour or two to save themselves from the first devastating attacks by the Luftwaffe, which could hardly be expected to honour the diplomatic immunity even of their fellow countrymen.

Whoever was to blame for it, the misunderstanding

between the Greek and British delegations at the meetings at Tatoi on 22 and 23 February wasted two precious weeks and doomed *Lustre* to failure. The British had assumed that the naturally strong Aliakmon line would be held by substantial Greek forces fighting shoulder to shoulder with all the troops that could be spared from North Africa. The Greeks had assumed that the decision to man the Aliakmon line was being held in suspense until Yugoslavia's position had been ascertained. At the beginning of March, by which time the full extent of the misunderstanding had become clear, the greater part of the Greek armies still remained on the Albanian front and in eastern Macedonia, leaving in the Aliakmon region only the newly-created Central Macedonian Army, which did not merit the name. It consisted of three divisions of third-rate troops with no modern equipment or transport; and it was with this ramshackle crew that the forces coming from North Africa – originally planned to be the 1st Armoured Brigade, the New Zealand Division, the 6th Australian Division, the Polish Brigade, and the 7th Australian Division – were to be asked to hold the Germans.

The arrangements for the reception of the British troops were discussed on 6 March by Wilson and Papagos. The Commander-in-Chief of 'W Force' as the combined British and Central Macedonian Army was to be designated, cannot have derived much encouragement from the state of affairs disclosed. For example, it was explained that it would be possible to increase the number of trains for the arriving British forces from two a day on 8 March to six from 15 March, after that date there would be no more coal and no more trains. In any case, there would be no ambulance trains at all for the *Lustre* troops since they were required for the Greek army. The position regarding weapons was no better. Anti-tank guns captured from the Italians were awaiting the fitting of breech-blocks, which were being specially made. 75-mm guns, badly-needed as anti-tank weapons, were still on the water from England. Skoda mountain guns would be provided – but only when new breech-blocks had been manufactured for them. If Wilson had ever believed that *Lustre* had a real chance of success, he must surely have been disillusioned at this meeting.[12]

Lustre's rank and file may have been assigned an impossible task; but at the other end of the chain of command the position was even more difficult. For nearly a month Wilson remained incognito and incarcerated in the British Legation at the behest of the Greek government, who had the extraordinary delusion that if his appointment was not announced the Germans would be fooled into thinking that they need not worry about the arrival in Greece of allied troops from North Africa. Since Greece and Germany were not at war, it was open to the staff of the German Legation in Athens to monitor the arrival of the British troops without let or hindrance, and to feed their findings to Berlin, so that the damaging Greek stratagem was entirely pointless. On 9 March the Legation transmitted a detailed report on the strength of the British forces in Greece as at 4 March, and they had not the slightest difficulty in bringing this up-to-date as further contingents arrived. On the other hand, Wilson, who was required to masquerade during his period of non-command as plain 'Mr Watt', was prevented from taking part in the formation of the forces under his command, or carrying out any reconnaissance of the unusual terrain over which they would be fighting, except for two or three days in a semi-official capacity just before his appointment was announced. This unbelievable performance, which for a vital month left the Commander-in-Chief with no troops, and the troops with no Commander-in-Chief, was yet another serious barrier to the success of *Lustre*.

Another factor, which all along had bedevilled the allies' efforts to help Greece, was the Greek government's persistent refusal to bring their armies back from Albania and Eastern Macedonia to man a shortened defensive line. General Papagos accepted without question that the move

[12] WO 201/52, ff. 30-2.

would be strategically sound, but it was politically difficult
to withdraw the Eastern Macedonian Army because the
troops would have to abandon their homes and families.
He was therefore always searching for reasons to leave
them where they were. On 10 March he claimed that the
firm stand taken by the Yugoslav government had induced
the Germans to pause.[13] However, he had actually brought
himself to the point of deciding to issue the necessary
orders to bring back the Eastern Macedonian Army, when
he learned about the Yugoslav coup. He immediately
decided that the German threat had receded again, and
his order was never issued, although the coup might have
provided a heaven-sent breathing-space in which the
Eastern Macedonian troops could be safely withdrawn.[14]

It is difficult to follow the movement of the allied forces
without the help of a relief map. The area in which the
opposing armies first met, and indeed the country for a
good many miles to the south, is rugged and mountainous.
The mountains are separated by valleys and plains through
which torrents and great rivers flow; and at the time of
the engagement their upper slopes were still deep in snow.
There were four main passes – at Veria, Edessa, and on
either side of Mount Olympus, so that the room for
manoeuvre by conventional armoured troops was strictly
limited. They could function effectively in the plains and
lower valleys; but in the defiles and mountain passes tanks
could hardly operate and artillery could be used only with
the greatest difficulty. This meant that the German attacks
had to be funnelled through a limited number of places
and that if the allies had had at their disposal a reasonable
number of troops well-armed and supported from the air,
and had been given time to prepare defences they could
probably have held out for a long time against superior
forces. The area most suitable for armour ran from Florina
to Kozani, which was behind the main allied line, and
could be reached from Yugoslavia. If the Germans could
establish themselves there the allies were at their mercy.

[13] WO 201/52, f. 27.
[14] *Ibid.* 72.

The 1st Armoured Brigade arrived at the Piraeus on 7 March and reached the forward area by 21 March. It was stationed in the plain between the river Axios and the Olympus-Vermion mountain range, with orders to fight a delaying action there, and to cover the preparation of demolitions. The New Zealand Division followed and took up a position stretching from the Aegean coast north of Katerini westwards along the south bank of the river Aliakmon. The Division, under the command of Major-General Sir Bernard Freyberg was concentrated by 2 April. There was a gap of several miles on their left. Thereafter the line, which ran through Veria, Kozani and Naousa, and then via Edessa up to the Yugoslav frontier, was supposed to be held by the Central Macedonian Army. It had been intended that the 6th Australian Division should support the Greeks in the region of Veria; but before they could fully establish themselves there those units which had arrived were diverted to meet the ever-increasing threat that the Germans would sweep through Yugoslavia and into the easy country beyond Florina.[15]

Wavell, whose passion for security had left the Prime Minister in a state of mystification at the end of 1940,[16] insisted that there should be no announcement that British troops had arrived in Greece – a curious line, since anyone who reflected seriously on the decision to send an expedition must have concluded that it was nine-tenths a political gesture the value of which would be enhanced by the widest possible publicity. Churchill pointed out that the Italians had referred in their communiqués to an increase in convoys to Greece, but had not admitted that British troops had landed there. He guessed that this was because they feared that the news would strengthen the resolve of the Yugoslavs, and might even lead them to attack the Italians in Albania. It seemed to him that there was a strong case for making an announcement; but he concluded, probably with some misgiving, that the War

[15] WO 201/72.
[16] See above, p. 53.

Cabinet must adhere to their decision to leave matters of this sort to be settled by those on the spot.

On 7 April – the day before the first contact was made with the Germans – the Luftwaffe struck a most damaging blow at the allies' communications with North Africa. The Piraeus, which was the main port for the disembarkation of *Lustre*, and would have carried the vast bulk of the supplies needed to maintain the expedition, was heavily dive-bombed. Several ships were hit, including the *Clan Fraser*, which was fully loaded with high explosive. She was set on fire, and in due course blew up. Many of the harbour installations were destroyed by the explosion, and the burning débris set several other ships on fire. It was suggested in the Inter-Service report on the campaign that the precautions for unloading dangerous cargoes were in-adequate; and it was indeed hinted that the disaster would not have happened 'had a suitable Senior British Naval Officer been appointed'. The *Clan Fraser* should either have been berthed at a safe distance from other shipping and unloaded by lighters, or towed away when she caught fire, not, it must be admitted, a particularly pleasant task. Although the Piraeus was under the control of the Greek authorities it was submitted that the Royal Navy should have stepped in and taken complete charge of the situation.[17]

It had been recognized all along that the Florina gap was likely to prove to be the Achilles heel of the allies' defensive system. A force known as the Amynteion Detachment was therefore charged with the task of covering the gap. At first it comprised the 27th New Zealand Machine Gun Battalion (less two companies), the 64th Medium Regiment, Royal Artillery, and the 3rd Royal Tank Regiment, and was commanded by Brigadier J. E. Lee; but it was reinforced after 8 April when the news came that Yugoslav resistance had collapsed. This news can hardly have surprised General Wilson. The only tangible result of Dill's visit to Belgrade had been a meet-

---

[17] WO 201/54; WO 201/45, f. 34.

ing with a representative of the Yugoslav General Staff
on 3 April at Florina, when Wilson concluded that the
Yugoslavs had neither the will nor the means to resist a
German invasion. It transpired at the same meeting that
the Yugoslav government had been under the impression
that the allies had brought five divisions from North
Africa, and when they learned the truth it can hardly have
strengthened their resolve.

Units of the 6th Australian Division, which had been
heading for the Veria Pass, were now ordered to join the
Amynteion Detachment. It was further reinforced by the
19th Australian Infantry Brigade (less one battalion); and
the command was taken over by Major-General I. G.
Mackay. The 1st Armoured Brigade blew the demolition
belts east of the Olympus-Vermion position, and withdrew
through the Edessa gap to join itself to the Amynteion
Detachment. It was hoped that this augmented force
would be able to hold the Germans entering from Yugoslavia long enough to enable the troops on the Olympus-
Vermion line to withdraw successfully; and it was accepted
that withdrawal was now inevitable. The weakening of
the already thin defensive line for the sake of strengthening the Amynteion Detachment meant that all hope of a
successful resistance in the forward position had now been
abandoned.

Contact was made with the Germans on 8 April when
units of the 1st Armoured Brigade encountered enemy
patrols on the river Axios. German patrols also reached
the neighbourhood of Veria and Edessa. Next day a small
party trying to row across the Aliakmon river was fired on
by the New Zealanders. On 10 April the threatened attack
on the Florina gap materialized. It was halted by artillery
fire from the Amynteion Detachment, and by the RAF,
which at this time was still able to help the ground forces
by bombing enemy columns on the roads. This was only
a temporary success, however, for the Germans built up
a concentration of infantry near Vevi and Kelli in front of
Amynteion, and on 11 April launched an attack with
tanks supported by infantry. It was beaten off with con-

siderable enemy casualties, but next day the Luftwaffe carried out a heavy raid on Kozani behind the position of the Amynteion Detachment, which revealed the shape of things to come. There was virtually no opposition to the raiding aircraft, and the town was severely damaged. Most of the inhabitants fled, accompanied by the police and the troops who were supposed to be guarding the town.

Although the Germans had been held for two days at Amynteion it was clear that the adjusted allied line – running from Katerini along the Aliakmon to Naousa, Mount Vermion, Podos, Kleidi, and Nymphaion – could not hold out much longer with the relatively small number of troops available; and it was decided to move further back. During this withdrawal the Central Macedonian Army began to collapse, and completely failed to carry out the role assigned to it by General Wilson. It was, for example, ordered to make its headquarters near to the Amynteion Detachment so that it would have access to the British communications system; but instead it hurried back to Vateron, many miles to the rear, where there was a single civilian telephone – if indeed the Central Macedonian Army wanted to make use of any telephone. The troops moved in disorganized groups 'which became indescribably jumbled' and whose main objective was to reach the comparative safety and comfort of Athens as quickly as possible.

On 13 April Wilson heard the news that Yugoslavia had capitulated and conferred with Major-General Sir Thomas Blamey, who was in command of the right sector of the allied line, about the next step. They considered that in the new circumstances, in which the Greek army had become a liability, there must be a further withdrawal to the Thermopylae line – running from the town of Molos on the Gulf of Euboea east of Thermopylae, to Eratine on the Gulf of Corinth. This was also a naturally strong defensive line, and had the merit that it was only fifty miles long (compared with the hundred miles of the Olympus-Vermion line) and could in theory at least be held by the British troops on their own. When this was put to General Papagos he agreed with alacrity, and indeed pressed Wilson to prepare to withdraw from Greece entirely, in order to avoid the devastation of the country.

The main problem which faced Wilson was how to conduct an orderly retreat with the limited number of troops at his disposal. He was anxious about his left flank, which was particularly vulnerable to pressure from the advancing Germans, and decided to protect it by forming a special force to block the routes leading from Grevena and Metsovon via Kalabaka into the Larissa plain. The 1st Armoured Brigade was now in a very weak state, and the plan was that the 17th Australian Brigade, which had only recently arrived and had not yet reached the front, and some other formations should be united under the command of Brigadier S. G. Savige. 'Savige Force' was complete on 14 April and the 1st Armoured Brigade began to move through it next day towards the Thermopylae line, where it passed under General Blamey's command. 'Savige Force' itself, having done its job, withdrew from the Kalabaka area on the night of 17/18 April.[18]

Dill reported to the War Cabinet on 14 April that the news from Greece was very serious; and the members sought to console themselves with reminders of the constant efforts that had been made to help the Greeks to save themselves by bringing back troops from Albania and the Bulgarian border. Churchill said that Britain was in no way to blame for the consequences of Greece's failure to heed her many warnings. The Greek government had asked for permission to establish themselves in Cyprus if they were forced to leave Greece. They considered it politically important to have a small piece of territory which in exile they could call their own. It was pointed out in the Cabinet discussion that there was a strong party in Cyprus which wanted the Island to be annexed by Greece, and that if the King was allowed to exercise jurisdiction over even a token area the Governor's position

[18] WO 201/72.

would become impossible. It was agreed that the King and his Ministers would be welcome in Crete in the first instance; and that the British government would be prepared to discuss the question of a move to Cyprus later.[19]

It is most unlikely that the allies' original forward line could have been held even if the Central Macedonian Army had been prepared to fight; but without any significant help from Greek troops the task was quite hopeless. Moreover the weather, which at first prevented the Luftwaffe from playing a full part in the German advance, improved and made it possible for the huge number of aircraft available to mount a continuous and intensive attack on the allies' vital road communications. Nevertheless, spirited delaying actions were fought by the British at strategic points, and the skilful use of demolitions kept the main German forces at a safe distance. The withdrawal to the Thermopylae line was successfully completed on 20 April. By this time the 1st Armoured Brigade had lost most of its tanks, not through enemy action but simply because of mechanical failure hastened by operations in most difficult country.

The Polish Brigade and the 7th Australian Division had not yet left North Africa, and their sailing was cancelled by Wavell on 16 April. He also ordered that ships on their way to Greece should turn back, that those in Greek ports not yet unloaded should return with their cargoes, and that those still loading for Greece should be unloaded. When he told London about these moves he asked for guidance as to what he should do about Papagos's suggestion that the British should leave Greece. After discussion in the Defence Committee on 16 April Churchill sent Wavell a peevish telegram complaining about the lack of news from the 'Imperial front in Greece', and saying that *Lustre* must not remain in Greece against the wishes of the Greek Commander-in-Chief; but it would be necessary first to get the government to endorse Papagos's request.[20]

[19] CAB 65/22, ff. 113-15.
[20] *Ibid.* 69/2 (16).

While the withdrawal to the Thermopylae line was still in progress a group came to Athens on 17 April from the Joint Planning Staff in Cairo to plan the evacuation of *Lustre*, which they had already been studying for some time. Next day the new Greek Minister President, Koryzis, whose ten-week term of office had seen the country reap the unhappy reward of his predecessor's prolonged attempt to appease the Germans, committed suicide. On 19 April Wavell went to Athens to confer with Wilson and Blamey. Between them they carefully argued out the case for staying on in Greece. It was always better to fight on, if possible. It would tie up large enemy forces, especially aircraft which might otherwise be used against Britain. Withdrawal would have a bad effect on morale, it would lead to the loss of men and equipment, and it would impose a severe strain on the navy.

There were, however, powerful arguments on the other side. The maintenance of *Lustre* for an indefinite period would also strain the navy's resources, and merchant shipping. The available aerodromes were very poor, and in any case it would be virtually impossible to replace RAF losses which it was estimated would be about thirty to forty aircraft a week. The Germans had at least 300 planes at their disposal, compared with the RAF's single squadron of Hurricanes, two of Blenheims, and one of Gladiators. Large army reinforcements would also be needed, and this might lead to a serious weakening of the allied position in North Africa. The Greek army was incapable of further resistance. The government, having lost its Minister President, did not seem to know its own mind. Finally, the allies would become responsible for feeding the Greek people.

The whole of this discussion was academic in the light of Wavell's decision to stop sending men and supplies to Greece, and it is difficult to understand why it took place. Even if Wilson and Blamey had wanted to fight on their hands were tied. Inevitably they agreed that *Lustre* must be withdrawn; and they reckoned that they would be lucky if they got 30 per cent of the men safely away.[21] The King had no hesitation in accepting Wavell's conclusion when he put it to him, accompanied by Wilson and Palairet, on 21 April.

It would have been unwise, in view of the overwhelming superiority of the Luftwaffe, to use the Piraeus or any of the alternative Greek ports for the evacuation; and in any case the Piraeus was virtually unusable as a result of the air raid of 7 April. Wavell therefore ordered that the troops should be got away on as wide a front as possible. Any who were cut off or were unable to embark from the chosen beaches were ordered to make for the Peloponnesus in the hope that they might be picked up after the main evacuation had been completed. Wilson chose 28 April as the first night of the evacuation, but the surrender of the Greek army in the Epirus meant that the Germans approaching from the west might cut off the British force well before that date. Embarkation-day was brought forward to 24 April, and it was hoped to complete the operation in three days.

According to Wavell's report everything went according to plan, thanks to the efforts of the Royal Navy and the handful of aircraft still able to fly, except for two incidents. At Nauplion 1,700 troops had to be abandoned because a merchant ship had been set on fire by bombing and prevented the rescuing destroyers from approaching the quay. A merchant ship carrying men from the same port was set on fire by bombs. Two destroyers which picked up the survivors were themselves sunk by bombs almost immediately, and about 700 troops were lost.

The other failure recorded by Wavell concerned an embarkation attempt at Kalamata in the south of the Peloponnesus, where a German force entered the town just as the embarkation was beginning. Although it was driven out and 150 prisoners were taken, the navy was not informed of this success and was therefore left with the impression that the town was still in the hands of the Germans. As a result of this breakdown in communications 8,000 troops, including reinforcements for the New

21 WO 201/72.

Zealand Division, were left behind. This unfortunate incident more than doubled the number of men who had to be abandoned, for of the total sent to Greece – just under 58,000 – 43,000 were safely re-embarked. This was an infinitely better figure than Wilson and his colleagues had been prepared for.[22]

The Australian and New Zealand governments, who had allowed their troops to be sent to Greece largely on the strength of the War Cabinet's apparent belief that *Lustre* had a reasonable chance of success (whatever that might have meant) were naturally apprehensive about their fate when they learned that they were being pushed back by the Germans. A telegram came from the Australian government on 18 April saying that the immediate evacuation of the Australian troops was essential. They agreed with the decision to hold Crete, but not with Australian troops, which they wanted to be reassembled as a self-contained corps. The Prime Minister dealt forthrightly with this proposition. There could be no question of withdrawing the Australian contingent separately; and he thought that the matter might be left safely to Menzies. He concluded by observing: 'Mr Bruce [the Australian High Commissioner in London, on whom the Australian government relied for advice in addition to Menzies] is not good when things are bad'.[23]

On 22 April the New Zealand Prime Minister asked Churchill to do everything possible to ensure a safe and rapid evacuation, should the need arise – not realizing that the decision to evacuate had already been taken. The Dominions Office provided a draft reply which did no more than curtly acknowledge Fraser's anxious telegram. When Churchill saw this masterpiece of wooden-headed drafting, which had it been sent would have imposed a new strain on Anglo-New Zealand relations, he swiftly drew his pen through it, and replaced it with some mollifying Churchillian prose. He thanked the New Zealand Prime Minister for his generous and courageous message,

[22] *Supplement to the London Gazette*, 2 July 1946, pp. 3423-3444.
[23] PREM 3 206/1, ff. 10, 15.

and expressed regret about the lack of information about the progress of *Lustre*. The War Cabinet itself had been kept short of information, which was understandable, given the swift and complicated nature of movements in Greece. The New Zealand and Australian troops had acquitted themselves in a glorious manner and had hit the enemy far harder than he had hit them. The troops were in their new defensive positions at Thermopylae, but he had no doubt that early re-embarkation would be necessary. All plans had been made for this operation some time ago; and New Zealand might rest assured that the safe withdrawal of the men would have precedence over any other consideration – except that of honour. 'I have so greatly admired the grandeur of the attitude of your government, and my thoughts turn many times a day to the fortunes of your one splendid New Zealand Division, and of my heroic friend Freyberg.'[24] Honeyed words, designed to keep the New Zealanders from fretting during the unpredictable days of the evacuation.

The War Cabinet conducted a brief inquest into the failure of *Lustre* on 28 April. Churchill said that they could congratulate themselves on the number of troops evacuated. He estimated that the total losses would not exceed 10,000 men. The concluding stages of the campaign had been a glorious episode in the history of British arms. The losses inflicted on the enemy had almost certainly exceeded those of *Lustre* – a more cautious estimate than he had given the New Zealand Prime Minister – in spite of the fact that the withdrawal had taken place almost entirely without air support. He had no regrets about the enterprise. It had made Yugoslavia an open enemy of Germany. It had caused a marked change in the attitude of the United States to the allied cause. He went on to say that they must now expect a period of great activity in the Mediterranean. Crete and Malta, and probably also West Africa and Gibraltar would be attacked. He was afraid that in the long run it might not be possible to hold Crete.

24 PREM 3 206/1, ff. 1-3, 6.

The reports prepared immediately after the evacuation summed up the lessons learned. They did not record that the task which *Lustre* had been assigned was political rather than military, and incapable of fulfilment; but there was the usual technical commentary on aspects of the expedition intended to improve the performance of similar future enterprises. For example, the demolition belts had been well planned and executed – with one exception. An officer had experimented on what he took to be an un-important girder of a bridge. This experimental explosion blew up the whole bridge while large numbers of the allies were still on the wrong side of it. The lesson to be learned was that the middle of a withdrawal was not the best time for experiments. Nearly all the demolitions cut off at least temporarily some of the Greek forces. This was the price that had to be paid if the German advance was to be delayed; but the Greek Higher Command tried to hold up demolition work until all Greek soldiers and civilian refugees had been safely withdrawn, and even issued orders about demolition 'observance of which would have prevented the army from leaving Greece'.[25]

The main weaknesses were poor discipline and in-efficient communications. Good discipline was maintained throughout by some units, and on the beaches it was often excellent; but many drivers abandoned their vehicles for hours on end when under aerial attack, thus blocking the narrow roads and slowing-up the whole withdrawal. There were reports of 'lamentable scenes of ill-discipline' at Larissa. Wireless operators were poorly-trained and their equipment unreliable. The cipher staff were badly over-strained so that many messages were wrongly transmitted. Maps were out of date. Flying maps had place names which differed from those used by the Greek army; and maps of neighbouring countries were scarce and inaccurate. The most important lesson related to the role of troop-carrying aircraft in modern warfare. Air Commodore D'Albiac, who had been in command of the outnumbered

[25] WO 201/72.

RAF in Greece pointed out that with the introduction of parachute troops, airborne landings, and glider operations a new dimension had been created. His views were given great weight by the Inter-Services Committee which conducted the inquest on *Lustre*; but their report was not completed until March 1942 and long before then the new dimension had appeared again – with even greater effect – in Crete.[26]

On the whole *Lustre* came out of the operation very creditably in the eyes of its Commander-in-Chief. Wilson admitted that morale had shown signs of weakening during the withdrawal, and that a number of technical weaknesses had revealed themselves. But the main target of his criticism was the Military Mission in Athens on the performance of which the success of *Lustre* had largely depended. It was pointed out that senior officers appointed to a Military Mission should be specially selected for the job, and that it was not enough that an officer should be able to speak the language of the country to whose army he was affiliated. The Military Mission in Athens had failed to represent the military picture either in Greece or in Yugoslavia. The state of the Greek army, particularly as regards its ability to move, was not adequately appreciated, nor was it appreciated that the Yugoslav army could last only a few days against the German advance. The Military Mission failed to supply *Lustre* with general information on Greece, especially with regard to roads and communications. Moreover the little information provided on these subjects proved to be inaccurate. The Mission should have been closed down as soon as *Lustre* arrived, and its staff absorbed in *Lustre* headquarters, leaving only a handful to deal with supplies to the Greek army from outside Greece. But since the Mission derived its being from the War Office in London not even the Commander-in-Chief, Middle East, could tamper with it. In future, however, a Military Mission should not be allowed to shelter behind its charter from London.[27]

[26] WO 201/54.
[27] *Ibid.* 72.

This criticism was well-founded; but it would not have helped to absorb the Mission in Force Headquarters. The damage had been done long before the decision to send an expedition to Greece. The Mission had had several months to brief itself on military affairs in Greece and the neighbouring countries, particularly Yugoslavia; and a big enough staff – nearly thirty officers – to do the job thoroughly. Had it kept the War Office and Middle East Headquarters properly informed, it seems more than likely that *Lustre* would never have sailed.

VI

1. Crete: Strategic considerations

The British and Germans alike saw quite early on in the war that the time might come when Crete would be strategically important. In May 1940 the Commanders-in-Chief in the Middle East were authorized to examine the case for occupying the Island, more to deny it to the Italians than because it might be of use to the allies; but Admiral Sir Andrew Cunningham, Commander-in-Chief of the Mediterranean fleet, told Wavell that Crete was so important to the navy that they should put themselves in a position to land a force there at short notice. Wavell agreed and ordered that a battalion should stand by at Alexandria, stipulating, however, that it must not embark without his personal authority. This contingency enterprise – Operation *Sparrow* – was cancelled in August when it was understood that the Greeks themselves would defend the Island.

The allies continued to worry about Crete. In October 1940, when it was suspected that Italy might declare war on Greece, Papagos was given a memorandum setting out a British plan to help the Island in the event of attack. This was based on measures *presumed* to have been taken by Greece, an indication that although Britain and Greece had been working closely together neither knew much of what was in the other's mind. The presumptions included that Heraklion aerodrome would be obstructed, that coastal observation points round the Island would be manned, and that the Greeks would list the equipment lacking in Crete – there being no guarantee that Britain would supply it. The help offered was not impressive. Bombers could be sent quickly, and naval forces within thirty hours. At this time the Chiefs of Staff toyed with the idea of taking a leaf out of the Germans' book and suggested to Wavell that officers in plain clothes might be smuggled into Crete to give the benefit of their advice to the local troops.

On 22 October the Greek General Staff told the British Service Attachés in Athens that they believed that the Axis had missed their chance of invading Greece that year. They were satisfied that the lateness of the season and the lack of preparations ruled out an immediate attack; but they were equally convinced that a combined German and Italian attack would be launched in the spring of 1941. Less than a week later Mussolini made his desperate throw and proved them wrong. The Directorate of Military Intelligence in London was equally wide of the mark when it suggested that the Duce must have had Hitler's full consent,[1] and that unless they were miraculously helped by the weather the Greeks would succumb in a matter of weeks or even days. It was nearer the truth when advising that the best thing that Britain could do would be to occupy Crete immediately. It would be strategically right and would have a useful effect on Turkey and Middle Eastern countries generally.[2]

As soon as the news of the Italian attack was known a battalion destined for Malta was diverted to Crete.[3] The Prime Minister told Eden, who was then in the Middle East that it was of great importance to retain a naval fuelling base at Suda Bay, and also the best aerodrome available in Crete, since the successful defence of the Island would be an invaluable aid to the defence of Egypt. On the other hand its loss to the Italians would aggravate the existing difficulties which the allies were experiencing in the Mediterranean. 'So great a prize is worth the risk and almost equal to successful offensive in Libya. Pray examine the whole problem with Wavell and Smuts.' Eden replied that there was complete agreement among the commanders in the Middle East about the importance of holding Crete.[4]

---

[1] But see pp. 38-9 above.
[2] WO 201/55.
[3] Code name *Action*. A second echelon which left Port Said on 4 November was known as *Assumption*. Later the whole enterprise was known as *Creforce*.
[4] PREM 3/308, ff. 23-6, 113.

An advance party of a few officers from the three Services was sent to Crete to make contact with the Greek commander and the local authorities. This mission, led by Colonel H. M. J. McIntyre and given the code name *Tyremiss*, immediately showed the same ineptitude which was later a feature of the military mission to Greece. Their first action was to tell the British Minister in Athens that the Greek commander was hopelessly inefficient and must be replaced, and secondly that the whole of the secret police in the island must be removed. The Minister properly took the strongest exception to this poaching on his preserves. He sent an angry telegram to Wavell saying that he had no idea who this fellow Tyremiss was, and trusting that he would be stopped from meddling in Greek internal politics. Wavell did not disclose to Palairet that there was no one of the name of Tyremiss under his command, nor did he remind the Minister that he had been consulted before the mission went to Crete. With a commendable show of loyalty towards the individual members of the mission he simply agreed that Tyremiss had no business to make such suggestions and that he was being reprimanded.[5]

Eden stressed the value of Crete in another talk with Wavell on 3 November. It would help to secure the eastern Mediterranean and provide a base from which to attack Italian troops bound for North Africa; but the fleet could not safely be kept at Suda Bay because of the lack of protection from submarines. Wavell, reluctant as ever to weaken his forces elsewhere, was satisfied that there was no danger of an attack by the Italians before they had overrun Greece; and also that once the Cretans were properly organized a single British battalion and anti-aircraft defences would be all that was needed.[6] The War Cabinet decided, however, that a naval base should be established at Suda Bay, and orders were given to send out boom defences and so on. It was accepted that the Italians would become aware of this move, and that they

[5] WO 201/55, 10a, 10b.
[6] PREM 3/308, ff. 16, 19.

might react to it by pressing home their attack in the Western Desert.

On 6 November the Greek government informed the British that they proposed to withdraw six of their nine battalions in Crete, since they were needed on the Albanian front. Needless to say, Wavell immediately objected. Although he considered it reasonable to restrict the numbers of British troops sent to Crete on the ground that the Island was in no immediate danger of attack he was at the same time prepared to deny the Greeks the right to move their own men from Crete to join in the life and death struggle against Italy. This is surely convincing proof that his sense of priority and willingness to take sensible risks were sadly at fault.[7]

Churchill at once agreed with the Greek request, except that he asked that one battery should be left behind to give time for a British replacement to arrive. He told Dill that it would be too bad 'if in consequence of our using Crete for our own purposes' the Greeks were denied their right to take their troops to the mainland; and he accepted that their departure made it essential to send British reinforcements. He sensed that Wavell was dragging his feet and being too complacent about the need for a strong garrison, and invited Dill to remind him that the Island was part of his command. He would *have* to spare men to garrison it. He must provide 'in meal or malt' three or four thousand more troops, which need not be fully equipped, and must not be units earmarked for any action impending in the desert. Yeomanry from Palestine would do, or even Poles! (Churchill's exclamation mark.) Arms and equipment should be rushed to Crete to enable the Greeks to form a new reserve division – it would be a crime to lose the Island because there was an insufficient bulk of forces there.[8]

Wavell's reply was typically uninspired and unforthcoming. Dominion troops could not be made available for Crete since the Australian and New Zealand governments

[7] WO 201/56, 13a.
[8] PREM 3/109, f. 161.

did not want their formations to be broken up. The Indian Brigade could not be sent because of the climate. Poland was not at war with Italy, so a special dispensation would have to be obtained from General Sikorski before Polish troops were used. He was seriously disturbed by the British weakness in Palestine. In short he was reluctant to send any more troops to Crete since it was better to run risks there than elsewhere in his command.[9]

Dill deemed it necessary to spell out the position more clearly. He told the Commander-in-Chief that His Majesty's Government considered it imperative that in all circumstances Crete must be held. The security of the Island was his responsibility in conjunction with the naval and air commanders-in-chief. It seemed clear that more than two battalions would be needed; and the Australian government was being approached for authority to draw on those of their troops which were not yet fully trained or equipped. This authority was given immediately.[10]

Stimulated by the CIGS's telegram Wavell paid a brief visit to the Island on 13 November. He reported that all was well, and that the troops were in good spirits. In spite of his misgivings he agreed to send further reinforcements; and he left a brigadier to study the defences.[11]

At the beginning of December Churchill was still expressing anxiety about the state of affairs in Crete. He asked Ismay 'exactly what have we got and done at Suda Bay i.e. troops, A.A. guns, coast defence guns, lights, wireless, R.D.F. [radio direction finding] nets, mines, preparation of aerodromes, etc?' He hoped to be assured that many hundreds of Cretans were now strengthening the defences and improving the aerodromes. On the same day – 1 December – in a memorandum for the Chiefs of Staff he observed that the fact that the allies were now established at Suda Bay entitled them to feel easier about Malta. So long as the navy could use Suda Bay as a base it was unlikely that there would be an attempt to invade

[9] WO 201/56, 33a, 64a.
[10] *Ibid.* 42a; PREM 3/109, f. 159.
[11] WO 201/56, 108a.

Malta. The strategic balance in the eastern Mediterranean had been changed.

The Prime Minister's confidence was without foundation. Crete could have been made impregnable, at small cost, had those directly concerned with the defence of the Island grasped its importance, and taken the necessary measures while there was still time. Alas, they did not.

The possibility that they would have to occupy Crete at some stage was in the German's minds in the spring of 1940 when they were contemplating a campaign in the Balkans; and again later in the year when the despatch of forces to help the Italians in Libya was being considered. General Halder, Chief of the German Army General Staff, believed that the Island was of great importance. If the Axis held Alexandria it would become much easier to supply Libya, but that depended on holding Crete, which in turn called for an assault from the air. General Paulus, Halder's deputy, agreed that Crete could be taken, but he was doubtful if it could be held.[12]

Jodl correctly guessed that if the Italians invaded Greece it would compel the British to occupy Crete. The remedy was for the Italians to capture Mersa Matruh, to attack the British fleet with all the power at their command, and to use their consequent naval supremacy to occupy Crete before the British got there. He had intended to put this proposition to the Italian Military Attaché in Berlin on 28 October, but their meeting was cancelled because of the news that the attack on Greece was already under way. On the same day, at his meeting with Mussolini at the Palazzo Vecchio in Florence, Hitler offered his partner an airborne and a parachute division to forestall the British in Crete. The Duce refused the offer on the ground that he considered Crete to be unimportant, but more likely because he was anxious that the conquest of Greece should be his and his alone.

[12] Halder, 24 April, 4 May, 25 October.

Three days later the first British troops arrived in the Island.

At the beginning of 1941 the German navy prepared a philosophical review of the general situation in the Mediterranean area, which, taking its line from Raeder, it regarded as being of vital importance. Italy needed freedom of movement by sea to feed her large population, but so long as they held their key positions in the Mediterranean the British could interfere with that freedom. Therefore Italy's real task must be the destruction of the British fleet. She must take the offensive, since experience had shown that the Luftwaffe on its own could not achieve that objective. The fact that the Italian fleet was relatively weak made it all the more necessary to attack, since history had shown that it often paid off to do so with numerically-inferior forces. In any case it was far better for ships to be sunk in battle at sea than destroyed in harbour – a noble sentiment which the Italian navy might or might not have echoed. If Britain was allowed to retain her bases in the Mediterranean it would have a decisive bearing on the course of the war; and as things stood only the Luftwaffe was capable of striking at these bases. They were, however, a long way from the aerodromes of Sicily and southern Italy, so that a decisive aerial attack, especially on Crete, the most distant, would be very difficult.[13]

Not only did possession of Crete strengthen the British position in the eastern Mediterranean in the eyes of the Germans (they could hardly be expected to divine that the allies would be so criminally foolish as to leave the Island virtually undefended) but it also brought their bombers within striking distance of the Romanian oilfields about which Hitler was extremely sensitive. Perhaps on the assumption that the Island *must* have been made impregnable, the Germans did not mention it during the preliminary discussions about Operation *Marita*, in spite of its potential danger to them. Nor was it mentioned in Führer Directive No. 18, which contemplated the occupa-

[13] MOD 50/789-803.

tion only of northern Greece, nor in Directive No. 20 which out of deference to the wishes of the navy and Luftwaffe substituted the whole of mainland Greece for the original more limited objective. Even in Directive No. 27 of 4 April the preamble of which records that since the Yugoslav forces are disintegrating, the Greek army in Thrace has been eliminated, and the Salonika basin and the area round Florina have been occupied, Greece now lies at the mercy of the Wehrmacht there is still no reference to the possibility of an attack on Crete, although a parachute operation against Lemnos and the occupation of Thasos and Samothrace are provided for.

It was not until 25 April that Hitler issued Directive No. 28 which said that Crete must be occupied to provide a base for aerial warfare against Britain in the eastern Mediterranean. This was supplemented by Directive No. 29 on 17 May – three days before Operation *Merkur* began. German objectives in the Balkans, which had been to drive the British from the peninsula, and to broaden the base for German air operations in the eastern Mediterranean, had been accomplished. The Italians would now be responsible for the occupation of Greece. Until Crete had been taken, however, it would still be necessary for the Wehrmacht to retain bases on the mainland of Greece from which the invasion forces would take off.

2. Forlorn hope

The report prepared in June 1941 by the Inter-Services Committee on the fall of Crete, whose job it was to be wise after the event and to ensure that the lessons learned were made available for the planning of future operations, reveals how the chance of making the Island impregnable was thrown away in the six months before the Germans attacked.

Wavell was no doubt right to regard Crete as being of secondary importance in 1940; but this did not mean that it should be almost totally neglected until further notice. That is really what happened. The appointment of Major-

General E. C. Weston, who went to Crete at the beginning of April 1941 to prepare for the establishment at
Suda Bay of a full naval base, was the sixth change of
command since the British troops arrived in November
1940. This surely reflects the Commander-in-Chief's lack
of interest, and indeed his failure to accept Churchill's
view that Crete might one day become a key point that
must be held at all costs. None of the commanders was in
post long enough to master the problem of the defences,
to recommend what should be done, and to ensure that it
was done. Although at one stage Wavell had it in mind
that a division might be needed to hold Crete, no related
defence plan was ever prepared. There was no attempt to
build field works or strong points in areas where static
defences were required, nor were beaches obstructed
against amphibious landings or crash landing aircraft.
'The task may have been Herculean', says the report, 'but
in the face of an industrious enemy Herculean tasks must
be faced'. In fact, the task was not superhuman. The men
were available, but they were not used. The time was
available, but it was frittered away. What was missing, in
spite of clear directions from the Prime Minister to the
higher command, was understanding of the problem, and
the will to solve it.

The Inter-Services Committee's report is a formidable
catalogue of failure. The role of the garrison was chopped
and changed, as well as its command. At first its task was
to defend the fuelling base at Suda Bay and in co-operation with the local Greek forces to defeat any attempt by
the enemy to gain a foothold in the Island. It is unlikely
that as then constituted it would have been strong enough
or well-trained enough to do this. Later its task was reduced to no more than the defence of Suda Bay, which
made rather better sense, given its numbers. Then at the
end of April 1941, when even Wavell saw that Crete was
likely to be moved into the front line, its role was redefined
as being to deny to the enemy the use of the air bases.[14]

[14] WO 201/2652, p. 15.

Had the Island's strategic worth been correctly evaluated, and had the appropriate garrison been provided – which could have been done without prejudice to the allies' position elsewhere in the region – it is virtually certain that the German assault would have failed.

There was no attempt to build up a reserve of tools, and one commander who planned an intensive programme of trench digging, which would have proved invaluable when the assault came, was actually discouraged.[15] There were no operational RAF units in the Island until the evacuation from Greece began, although even a token force would have gained useful experience and been able to point to some of the weaknesses which appeared only at the eleventh hour when it was too late to do anything about them. During the period of the occupation the RAF personnel were concerned mainly with administrative problems. The Senior Air Officer, Crete, was no more than a Flight Lieutenant whose seniority and experience were totally inadequate, having regard to the lack of guidance which he was given as to policy and requirements generally. Although an attempt was made to construct or improve seven aerodromes, shortage of constructional equipment, tools, and vehicles made reasonable progress impossible. There was no attempt to provide satellite landing grounds, although there was plenty of scope for them. There were aircraft pens only at Heraklion, where pens designed for bombers had been adapted to take two fighters each; and there were none at all at Maleme and Retimo, where aircraft had to be hidden in nearby olive groves. At Heraklion the aircraft fuel dump was outside the defence perimeter, which indicated a singular lack of initiative on the part of the local air and military commanders.[16]

The catalogue runs on almost indefinitely. There was confusion over the supply of fuel to the RAF and Fleet Air Arm, because of inadequate planning and liaison

[15] WO 201/2652, p. 17.
[16] *Ibid.* 55, f. 12.

between the two. There was no serious attempt to improve communications in the Island, and the inadequate operational lines were put out of action as soon as the attack started, which greatly impaired the value of both fighter and anti-aircraft defences. Not everything had been neglected, however. The navy had succeeded where the RAF and the army had failed. The naval defences of Suda Bay had been brought up to a satisfactory standard; but the efficiency of the navy could not begin to compensate for the failures of the other two services.

The scene was now set for as hopeless, unnecessary, and gallant a defensive operation as British troops were ever condemned to undertake.

It is ironic, having regard to Wavell's extreme reluctance to send troops to Crete, that the greater part of the British troops there on the eve of the German attack had in effect been installed by the Wehrmacht. Although some months earlier Wavell had reckoned that a single British battalion would be enough to hold the Island, there were now nearly 29,000 men in the garrison, of whom nearly 20,000 had been swept from Greece by the Germans. The basic garrison consisted of about 5,000 men of the original *Action* and *Assumption* forces, and 3,500 reinforcements from Egypt. Although the total numbers are impressive the men who had been evacuated from Greece were exhausted, poorly fed, and very badly equipped.

The Germans studied two alternative plans of attack. They had no adequate naval forces in the Mediterranean, and they could not rely on the Italian navy. This meant that Crete could be captured only from the air. One plan was that the western end of Crete from Maleme to Canea should be first occupied and that airborne infantry should move out from this sector to capture the rest of the Island. This had the advantage that substantial forces could be thrown initially into a limited area and very quickly gain control of it; but it had the serious disadvantage that the second stage of the operation would be made very difficult by the shape of Crete. Troops moving along the narrow coastal strip would be very vulnerable to attack from the mountains running the whole length of the Island.

The alternative plan was to attack seven important objectives simultaneously, so that the whole objective would be attained in one fell swoop; but the danger of this was that the attacking forces would be widely dispersed and some of the individual assaults might fail to consolidate their position and link up with their neighbours. When the two plans were put to Göring he found it difficult in the absence of definite information about the strength of the garrison to decide which was the better; and he ended up with a compromise under which four main objectives would be attacked. It was believed that this would reduce the risks in the other plans to an acceptable level. By seizing these four points in turn the attacking forces would have the benefit of the maximum protection from the Luftwaffe. Maleme and Canea were to be captured in the morning, and Retimo and Heraklion in the afternoon. As soon as the airborne attack succeeded a seaborne expedition would bring substantial reinforcements.

General Freyberg, who was given command of the garrison was faced with the same sort of choice. Should he disperse his forces with a view to protecting the aerodromes against airborne attacks and the beaches in their vicinity against landings from the sea; or should he concentrate on defending the three aerodromes which were operational, and the Suda Bay base? In the event he decided on dispersal, which led to particular difficulty west of Canea where there were twelve miles of beach to defend.

There was little to do now but to sit and wait for the arrival of the Germans. The War Cabinet had no doubt that an attack was imminent, and believed that it would be both airborne and seaborne. It was estimated that 3,000 paratroops might be involved in the first sortie, but if gliders were used the number might be as high as 4,000; and there might be two or three sorties a day. There were probably 315 long-range bombers in the Balkan area;

sixty twin-engined fighters; 270 single-engined fighters; 240 dive bombers; 200 transport aircraft near Plovdiv, and another 100 in the heel of Italy.[17] These were establishment figures, however, which was not made clear when they were passed to Crete. The number of serviceable aircraft was reckoned to be only half the establishment, so that the enemy threat was made to appear twice as great as it really was.[18]

On 29 April Churchill telegraphed to Wavell telling him that the information available in London suggested that the Germans would attack very soon, and added: 'Let me know what forces you have in the Island and what your plans are. It ought to be a fine opportunity for killing the parachute troops. The Island must be stubbornly defended.'[19] It was of course entirely necessary that the intelligence gathered in London about enemy dispositions and intentions in the whole of the Balkans and Middle East should be passed to the Commander-in-Chief, but a line should have been drawn there – if Middle East Command enjoyed the government's confidence. Churchill, however, could not be kept out of the battle. It occurred to him that the garrison might be short of maps of Crete. A flurry of minutes was created to satisfy him on the point, culminating with one from the CIGS assuring him that it could be safely assumed that there were plenty of maps and that they were up-to-date. This was not good enough for the Prime Minister, who said he feared that any Germans who reached Crete would be better informed about it than the garrison. Enquiries must be made on the spot.[20]

Churchill also thought that an attempt should be made to land a few tanks on the Island before the battle began, and proposed that the *Clan Fraser*, which was en route for Alexandria, should be diverted to disembark twelve tanks. The Chiefs of Staff objected on the ground that she

[17] PREM 3/109, ff. 154-6.
[18] AIR 8/545.
[19] PREM 3/109, f. 152.
[20] *Ibid.* ff. 131, 132, 137.

was also carrying field guns, Hurricanes, and ammunition which should not be put at risk by diverting her to Crete. It was therefore suggested that the first twelve tanks to be unloaded at Alexandria should be sent at once to Crete. When this was put to Wavell he replied that he had already arranged to send six infantry tanks and fifteen light tanks.[21]

Not content with seeking to ensure that the garrison was adequately equipped, Churchill sought to lay down the tactics which should be employed in Operation *Scorcher*, as the defence of the Island was code-named. The aerodromes should be allowed to fall easily into the hands of the enemy parachutists, and when the airborne landings began special assault parties in concealment nearby should burst out and destroy the intruders. He asked that a special officer should be sent to Freyberg to show him recent papers on this subject – which would then be destroyed by fire. The officer would be answerable for the destruction of the papers in the event of engine failure en route. The Prime Minister did not go so far as to specify the means of destruction to be used in such an emergency, but since fire would almost certainly be discouraged in an aircraft about to make a forced landing, it may be presumed that he would have been required to eat them. This, and other suggestions were put to Wavell by the Chiefs of Staff (who at least had the grace to admit that they were handicapped by lack of local knowledge). The Commander-in-Chief agreed to send the special officer and to pass on the other points to Freyberg; but added, reasonably, that the details of the defence of the Island must be left to the local commander.[22]

The Prime Minister continued to keep up the pressure. On 14 May he telegraphed Wavell saying that he assumed that he was keeping in the closest touch with the commanders-in-chief of the navy and air force; and he followed this next day asking for an assurance that all possible

[21] PREM 3/109, f. 123.
[22] *Ibid.* ff. 119, 120, 123.

reinforcements had been sent to Crete. Wavell replied patiently that he *was*, and they *had*.

The muted misgiving which the New Zealand government had expressed on the eve of the expedition to Greece now manifested itself again – hardly surprisingly, since they were concerned with the sensible deployment of the New Zealand Division, yet had no real control over its destiny. When Freyberg reported to them that he was to command in Crete, and gave a gloomy appreciation of the situation – insufficient tools for digging, little transport, inadequate equipment and ammunition, his aircraft outnumbered by forty to one, few ships to meet a seaborne invasion – they had little difficulty in concluding that the situation was grave. Their Prime Minister asked Churchill either that the troops should be given the means to defend themselves, or that the decision at all costs to defend Crete – the strategic importance of which was fully recognized – should be reversed.[23]

This extremely sensible communication put Churchill on his mettle and gave rise to a personal and secret reply full of honeyed comfort which did not bear critical analysis. He was glad that the exigencies of the evacuation should have carried the New Zealand Division, after its brilliant fighting in Greece, in such good order to Crete, the defence of which was one of the most important factors in the defence of Egypt. The successful conclusion of the evacuation, after inflicting so much loss on the enemy, and paying the allies' debt of honour to Greece, had been an inexpressible relief to the Empire. Any seaborne attack on Crete would be small, and the navy would dispose of it. An airborne attack would suit the New Zealanders down to the ground since they would be able to fight man to man against an enemy without mechanical advantages. If the Germans landed, it would be the beginning, not the end, of their embarrassment. Crete was mountainous and wooded and would give peculiar scope to the qualities of the New Zealand troops.[24] The under-

[23] PREM 3/109, f. 142.
[24] *Ibid.* ff. 139-40.

lying suggestion that the New Zealanders were a race of super-aboriginals living in woods and mountains, thirsting for blood, does not seem to have upset Fraser unduly; but whatever he made of it, the fundamental point was clear. However badly placed was the garrison, there was to be no question of withdrawing it without a fight. For the second time in a matter of months the misgivings of the New Zealand government did not have the attention they deserved.

German aerial attacks on Crete and shipping bound for the Island began on 1 May; and the airborne offensive followed on 20 May after intensive bombing at dawn. It is not possible here to give an account of the bitter fighting over the next ten days – admirable descriptions can be found in the British and New Zealand official histories. There is no doubt that the deciding factor was the Germans' overwhelming superiority in the air; and equally there is no doubt that they achieved victory so narrowly and at such enormous cost that had the garrison been able to draw on even a minimal amount of fighter defence it would almost certainly have turned the scales in their favour. When the German troop carriers and gliders were making their ponderous way to the landing places they presented the easiest of targets and would have suffered very heavily at the hands of even a few fighter pilots. On 19 May there were in Crete seven fighters fit for operational use, and it was decided by the Senior Air Officer, in consultation with Freyberg, that they should be sent away to safety. Had these fighters been available next day when the German attack was launched it must have greatly affected the balance of power, and perhaps changed the whole course of the battle.[25]

The Germans modified their original plan to attack their four objectives in succession during the day, and attacked Maleme and Suda simultaneously in the morning, and Heraklion and Retimo simultaneously in the after-

[25] WO 201/99, f. 21.

noon. They suffered disastrous losses and failed to establish a significant foothold anywhere except at Maleme, where they concentrated in the bed of the river Tavronitis. Here the defenders were caught by surprise. They had been on the lookout for paratroops but the first to land, masked by huge dust clouds caused by the earlier bombing, were glider-borne troops who arrived much more quickly than paratroops could do; and then provided covering fire for the paratroops who came almost on their heels. During the day more and more troops poured in, troubled little by the anti-aircraft defences which had been seriously weakened by the bombing, and troubled not at all by allied aircraft.[26] Nevertheless it was clear by nightfall that the Germans had completely failed to attain their objectives, and that their seaborne invasion which was timed to start as soon as the airborne troops were established would have to be postponed. In the event the element of the seaborne invasion destined for Maleme put to sea late in the evening of 21 May, and was intercepted by the Mediterranean Fleet which, in spite of incessant attacks by dive bombers during the hours of daylight, had been waiting for it. The Fleet had its revenge and inflicted heavy losses on the invasion force before it turned tail. Next day, however, the dive bombing began again. Two cruisers and a destroyer were sunk, and several other ships hit. In the early hours of 23 May Admiral Cunningham gave the order to withdraw, his decision being partly based on a signal that the battleships were short of anti-aircraft ammunition – which later turned out to be untrue. This singular mischance – which was paralleled by similar misunderstandings in Crete itself – may have been a blessing in disguise, for before the Fleet could get beyond the range of the dive bombers two more destroyers were sunk.

Freyberg's forces were now on their own. They had no

[26] On 23 May a handful of Hurricanes fitted with extra fuel tanks at the expense of much of their armament reached Crete from Egypt, but they were too few and too slow because of their modifications to be of any real help.

aircraft and no ships to help them. The enemy could come across the sea and through the sky in his own good time with all the strength he cared to muster. It was only a question of waiting until the defenders' daily losses exceeded those they inflicted on the attackers – a variant of the law of diminishing returns – after which further resistance would become pointless. On 27 May the order was given to withdraw from the Island, and on 30 May the last evacuation ship left. Roughly 15,000 men were taken safely to Egypt. 14,000 remained behind, killed, wounded or taken prisoner.

Estimates of the cost of the German success in terms of casualties vary greatly. Freyberg put the total figure for killed, wounded and missing at 17,000, which was certainly far too high. The official German record shows that the total losses of the army and Luftwaffe were 6,453, including nearly 2,000 killed. It has been suggested that a realistic estimate of the total killed would be round about 8,000.[27] Writing in 1972 Admiral Walter Ansel says that 3,986 Germans were killed, 2,594 wounded, and seventeen taken prisoner. His estimate for the allied side is 4,051 killed, of whom 2,000 were sailors, 1,738 wounded, and 12,254 taken prisoner, which gives about 16,000 allied killed and taken prisoner, compared with the German figure of 4,000.[28]

Whatever the precise truth, the fact is that the German losses were so unexpected and staggering that they may have convinced Hitler that air operations of this sort should not be repeated. General Student, who commanded the assault on Crete, saw it as the first phase of an airborne offensive, with the Suez Canal as its ultimate goal, Cyprus and Malta having been captured en route; and he believed that Hitler was moved by German losses in Crete to discourage airborne assaults on the grand scale. It seems more likely, however, that Hitler's decision to draw the line at Crete was due to his wish to give priority to the

[27] Buckley, p. 293.
[28] Ansel, p. 419.

invasion of Russia, rather than to the statistical disaster of *Merkur*. If he had been convinced that he would win the war by first winning the Mediterranean he would not have found it difficult to commit there the millions of lives which he threw away in Russia.

VII

Conclusion

If Mussolini had not, in October 1940, made his desperate
bid to achieve an hour of glory at small cost, the Greek
government's policy of appeasement would have kept both
the Germans and the British at arm's length from Greece.
The allies would not have been given the chance to help
themselves by helping the Greeks, nor would there have
been any question, at least in the foreseeable future, of
their taking the initiative and landing in Greece uninvited.
They had too few troops to mount their own campaign in
the Balkans, even if it had seemed profitable. But the
Duce *did* intervene in Greece, in the interests of his own
immortality, and was rewarded with a resounding military
disaster. It set up strategic shock waves that could have
started a general Balkan war and endangered the Germans'
right flank in their impending attack on Russia – had not
Operation *Marita* dampened them down.

That operation was everything that Mussolini's *Emergenza G* was not. It had a positive and necessary objective
– to control the Balkans and thus repair the strategic damage inflicted on the Axis cause by Mussolini's stupidity.
It was planned with meticulous care by professionals who
knew what they were doing, and was timed with due attention to the campaigning season. It was carried out with
overwhelming force and utter ruthlessness. It achieved its
objective quickly and efficiently. German casualties may
have been high, but they were acceptable. It is true that
Hitler had to postpone his attack on Russia for a month
or so, but he was well aware that this price would have to
be paid when he ordered the invasion of Yugoslavia and
Greece. He calculated that he could take the delay in his
stride, and he was right.

The Führer's mistake was not that he weakened his
assault on Russia by taking time off to dispose of the
Yugoslavs, the Greeks, and the British expeditionary

force, but rather that he embarked on *Barbarossa* at all. Had he instead followed Raeder's advice and gone all out to win control of the whole Mediterranean he would almost certainly have succeeded, and Britain would almost certainly have lost the war before the United States could come effectively to her rescue. It is ironic that the Duce's invasion of Greece, irresponsible though it was, pointed the way to a quick Axis victory. Had Hitler followed his partner south into the Balkans – leaving his eastern frontiers well guarded – and kept on going, he might have won the war within a year.

Italy and Germany both made mistakes in the Balkans. What of Britain? Churchill, at least, must have very quickly seen how grievous the allies' strategic miscalculation had been. He must have recognized that the successes claimed for *Lustre* – the upsetting of the Germans' timetable, and the favourable effect on public opinion in the United States – were far outweighed by the loss of men, weapons and equipment, and by the damage to morale. It is entirely reasonable that he should have dressed up a foolish and costly strategic move as a near success at a time when the nation needed all the encouragement he could provide. Had the rank and file who suffered in Greece, or the citizens for whom they were fighting appreciated that *Lustre* was a first-class strategic blunder it must surely have shaken their confidence in the abilities of their military leaders and the elected governments that directed them.

When writing about the Greek campaign Churchill says that he has recorded events as they occurred and action as it was taken. 'Later on these can be judged in the glare of consequences; and finally, when our lives have faded, history will pronounce its cool, detached, and shadowy verdict.'[1] Eden has accepted that mistakes were made. At one time he intended to write jointly with Wavell an account of the political and strategic aspects of the campaign, but this project was stopped by Wavell's death in

[1] Churchill, vol. iii, p. 207.

1950. Only a draft preface, in which they set their terms of reference, survives.[2] It says 'That mistakes were made, both in the political and military spheres, will be admitted . . .' Eden's humble admission and Churchill's sobering invitation make it rather more difficult to give the verdict which a dispassionate examination of the facts now suggests – that *Lustre* was an unnecessary and disastrous enterprise which brought virtually no profit and a great deal of loss.

Mussolini's miscalculation is obvious and understandable. It arose simply from overweening personal ambition. Hitler's was equally simple. His decision not to conquer the Mediterranean was entirely personal. The British decision was different. It was arrived at collectively by the War Cabinet after much advice from the Foreign Secretary, the Defence Committee, the Chiefs of Staff, the commanders in the field, and British diplomatic missions, and with the benefit of intelligence gathered from 'most secret sources' all over the Balkans and the Middle East. That it was a wrong decision may therefore be regarded as less forgivable; but this is no doubt the price which must be paid from time to time in a democracy.

Since it involved three sovereign governments it was a decision of unusual difficulty. Australia and New Zealand had to take a good deal on trust. Whatever their own assessment of the strategic value of the operation, it was virtually impossible for them to oppose a recommendation of the British War Cabinet.

Even if the decision was right at the moment when it was made (which is questionable) it very quickly became wrong, *before* the allies were irrevocably committed to it. Someone should have recognized the fact before it was finally implemented. The decision was reached on 24 February on the basis of the existing balance of power in the Balkans, and Eden's advice, which was given on the assumption that the Greeks would man the Aliakmon line forthwith. On 1 March the balance of power suddenly

[2] Eden, pp. 567-8.

changed when the Germans took over Bulgaria. On 2 March Eden discovered that the Greeks were not moving to the Aliakmon line, and in spite of this, renewed the allies' commitment to *Lustre* on his own initiative, without any attempt to seek the agreement of the Dominion governments. Australia and New Zealand resented having their troops committed by a British Cabinet Minister, but fell in with what was proposed, albeit with greater misgiving than before. The balance was now against *Lustre*, but Wavell's optimistic and misleading assessment of the North African situation arrived most inopportunely and turned the scale. Had he instead accurately foreseen what was going to happen in the most important area under his command it seems inevitable that the War Cabinet would have immediately abandoned the expedition to Greece.

There is no doubt that the Foreign Secretary played the biggest part in making the *Lustre* decision. He was present in the Middle East, and was therefore better placed than his colleagues in the War Cabinet to understand the implications of the proposed operation. In their discussions they must have weighted his telegraphed advice accordingly.

He had the opportunity at the meetings with the Greek government at Tatoi on 22 and 23 February of insisting that if a British force came to Greece it should man the line which his military advisers considered to be defensible and that the Greek armies must be withdrawn to it as a condition of British help. He did not so insist; and by offering to find out where the Yugoslavs stood he made it easy for the Greeks to do nothing.

The substantial difference of opinion as to what had been agreed at Tatoi emerged when he returned to Athens on 2 March. The British believed that the Greeks had agreed to withdraw immediately, and on this understanding they had begun to move troops from North Africa. The Greeks excused their failure to withdraw – according to the British account – on the grounds that morale would suffer in Albania, that there would be panic in Macedonia when the troops left, and that the withdrawing armies would be overtaken by the Germans; but their main defence was that it had been agreed that the withdrawals should not start until it was known whether the Yugoslavs would come in. The British representatives claimed that there had been no question of waiting to hear from Yugoslavia because there was no time.

Papagos claimed equally positively that he had insisted that before a large part of Greece was abandoned to the enemy without a shot being fired the attitude of Yugoslavia must be clear. The decision to withdraw from Macedonia and Albania would depend on Prince Paul's reply to Eden's telegram. He had repeatedly asked General Heywood after Eden left Athens if a reply had come from Belgrade to enable him to take the decision to withdraw.[3] This is a strong point in favour of the Papagos version. Heywood had attended the Tatoi meetings. He must have been aware of the conclusion as understood by Eden on 23 February; and it must have been obvious to him and his numerous colleagues that no order to withdraw had been issued. If the Greeks were thus falling down on a commitment of enormous importance to the British expeditionary force why did the Military Mission fail to report this vital fact to Eden and the CIGS? This was precisely the sort of task they existed to perform. There are two possible explanations. Either General Heywood agreed with Papagos's understanding of the conclusions of the Tatoi meetings; or the Military Mission completely fell down on the job.

With regard to the second alternative, it must be borne in mind that General Wilson wrote off the Military Mission as being useless, so perhaps they *did* fail to grasp the significance of Papagos's repeated enquiries.

It is not easy to adjudicate thirty years after the event, especially without the Greek record of the Tatoi meetings. The one thing that stands out is the extraordinary fact that the minutes of a meeting between two governments

[3] Papagos, pp. 323-4.

with so much at stake should be so ambiguous; and it says
little for the clarity of the discussions or the perspicacity
of those who recorded them. Papagos's alleged proposition
that it had been agreed to await Yugoslavia's decision was
a continuation of the Greek policy of putting off the evil
day, which dated back to Metaxas, and was bound sooner
or later to deliver the Greek army into the hands of the
Wehrmacht without a struggle. This may have been
stupid, but it is at least understandable.

It is more difficult to deduce what the British side had
in mind. If Eden left Athens after his first visit under the
impression that the Greeks had agreed to move their
troops to the Aliakmon line forthwith, that is to say if
Papagos's proposal had *not* been accepted, what then was
the point of asking Paul where he stood? Did the Foreign
Secretary envisage that if he agreed to side with the allies
the withdrawing Greek troops would then about face and
retrace their footsteps to a line nearer their borders? If
so, surely there would have been some discussion of such
a contingency plan at Tatoi; but there was none.

Eden's fundamental mistake, however, was not that he
hazarded the whole success of *Lustre* on a confused discussion but that he imagined that the Yugoslav army
might be capable of resisting a German advance. His
advisers were of course also to blame. The British Service
Attachés in Belgrade and the Military Mission in Athens
should have known just how weak the Yugoslav army was,
and they should have left Middle East Command in no
doubt on the point. As it was, the British discovered that
they had been seeking to ally themselves with a lost cause
only on 3 April when General Wilson met representatives
of the Yugoslav General Staff, by which time the greater
part of *Lustre* had arrived in Greece. The Yugoslavs had
virtually no tanks, no anti-tank weapons, and no anti-
aircraft guns; and above all no stomach for a fight with
the Germans. It was revealed at the same meeting that
the Yugoslavs were misinformed about the strength of
Lustre, which they had been led to believe would have as
many as five divisions. Thus, even if they had decided to

join the allies, it is possible that at the eleventh hour they would have changed their minds. It is also possible that if Eden had achieved the alliance with Yugoslavia for which he strove so hard that the British troops would have established themselves on the Nestos line, and the whole of *Lustre* would have been trapped by the German drive through unresisting Yugoslavia.

There is not the slightest doubt that on 22 February Eden should have struck a firm bargain with the Greeks, without an incomprehensible contingency clause. The British force would man the Aliakmon line, fighting shoulder to shoulder with the withdrawn Greek armies. If the Greeks had not been prepared to accept this ultimatum, he should at once have advised the War Cabinet to cancel *Lustre*.

Churchill's contribution to the decision-making process is curious. A leader must have flexibility of outlook, but the border between flexibility and vacillation, or simple acceptance of the latest advice proffered, is shadowy. In November 1940 when Eden seemed to be dragging his feet about helping Greece Churchill demanded instant action. Safety first was the road to ruin in war. Three months later their roles seemed to be reversed. Eden wanted to send troops to Greece and Churchill told him he must not feel obliged to do so – although success there would certainly be valuable. On 24 February he informed the War Cabinet that pending their decision he had given instructions for the expedition to be prepared. On 4 March he suggested that they might like to wait for a few days before taking a final decision. On 6 March he telegraphed Eden in Cairo saying that Greece must not be urged into a hopeless resistance in which Britain could not help her much, and that grave issues were now raised by the proposed use of Dominion troops. He was preparing him for news of a War Cabinet decision that troops would *not* go to Greece; but Eden's telegram of 7 March finally persuaded him the other way. He was deeply impressed by the Foreign Secretary's steadfast attitude. It was perfectly proper for the Prime Minister to change his mind day by day having regard to the changing situation; but some of his changes of opinion were less understandable.' At one moment the loss of Athens would be as serious a blow as the loss of Khartoum and less reparable. At another it would hardly matter.

The War Cabinet agreed that *Lustre* should go ahead on the assumption that it had a reasonable chance of success. This was never clearly defined but it probably meant that the Germans would be held somewhere in Greece, perhaps for years, until the allied line was able to move forward in the final campaign to annihilate the Wehrmacht. The expedition would also show the world, in particular the United States, that Britain was prepared to stand by her allies; but this was a fringe benefit. Churchill assured the Dominion governments that *Lustre* was not founded on *noblesse oblige*. It follows therefore that its success must be measured simply by the extent to which it held up the Germans in Greece – and whether in terms of men and equipment it showed a profit having regard to German losses.

The military commanders, no less than Churchill, must have seen very early on that their task was quite beyond them, that all they could do was to go through the motions of confronting the Germans, and then to withdraw with the smallest possible loss. What little chance they had of stemming the German advance was diminished by two factors for which the British side were themselves to blame.

In the first place the War Cabinet consistently took the view that the allies must not intervene in Greece except at the express invitation of the Greek government. This was very noble and may have gained the admiration of friendly neutrals; but it contrasts markedly with the attitude of the Germans towards their 'allies'. Hungary, Romania and Bulgaria were bribed, bullied and black-mailed into toeing the German line. Yugoslavia was smashed into submission. By playing to different rules Britain put herself at a disadvantage, which may seem to be foolish for a country fighting for her life. It is small consolation after defeat to say that at least one played fair. Her painfully correct attitude stemmed from Churchill; and it seems likely that he might have been less solicitous of Greek feelings if he had seen clearly that *Lustre* was likely to achieve something worth while. He may have felt instinctively that the expedition must fail, and that by putting the onus on Greece to ask for help he was providing a cushion against future criticism. Churchill made no bones about the fact that British troops were sent to Crete for Britain's own purposes, which suggests that he drew a distinction between Crete and the mainland. Crete was strategically important. The mainland of Greece was not. If this was so, then *noblesse oblige* was the only justification for *Lustre*, in spite of the fact that the Prime Minister consistently denied it.

Secondly, this voluntary subordination of the allies' self-interest strengthened the Greeks' hand in other respects to the detriment of the allies' position in the field. In particular it allowed them to remain under the extraordinary delusion that if they did nothing to provoke the Germans they would be allowed to remain at peace with the senior partner of the Axis while they drove the junior partner out of Albania. They maintained their make-believe position for over four months in spite of the fact that their friendly approaches to the Reich were regularly snubbed. The Germans made it perfectly clear that they had no intention of intervening in the conflict between Italy and Greece; and for the Greeks to think that they would refrain from joining in the war against them was wishful thinking of the most foolish kind. There was no point in Germany's formally declaring war in support of Mussolini until she was ready to move her troops south. Indeed to do so would have been damaging, for so long as Germany and Greece remained on speaking terms it was possible for German diplomats and Service Attachés to move freely about Athens gleaning information about the comings and goings of British Service personnel, and to make full use of the common intelligence network of the diplomatic community.

The practical effect of trying to appease the Germans long after there was any possible case for it was that the RAF was denied access to the most suitable bases for air operations, and that the despatch of British military assistance early in 1941 was vetoed. The most ludicrous consequence was the agreement that the commander-in-chief of *Lustre* should remain incommunicado and anonymous for the first month of his command. The inquest on *Lustre* dealt faithfully with this particular nonsense:

> It is not in the best interests of a campaign that the Force Commander should be kept apart from his troops and his H.Q. Yet from 5 March, when the first flights began to arrive, until 5 April there was no official Commander. The main reason for this was to delude the Germans into thinking that the British contingent was not ready to take the field since its commander was not appointed. Such a reason may have been excellent, but its effect upon the formation and organization of the Force was profound and rendered the task of the Staff of Force H.Q. extremely difficult. In point of fact the Germans knew all about Mr. Watt [General Wilson's code name] through their excellent Intelligence Service in Athens, while he himself was prevented for a whole month – more than half the period in Greece – from visiting Commanders and their troops and from carrying out essential reconnaissance at the front and elsewhere.[4]

The magnitude of the error of judgement in allowing *Lustre* to go ahead when it did is illustrated by the chronology of the expedition. When the first troops reached their forward positions in the Olympus-Vermion line it was immediately decided that they had not enough time to prepare defences before the Germans came on them, nor enough strength to man them if they had been prepared. In his report on the expedition after it had been withdrawn General Wilson astonishingly describes this forward line as a temporary position, which confirms the suggestion made above that wittingly or unwittingly all that the expedition could do was to make a token appearance before the Germans, and then pack its bags and

[4] WO 201/72.

retreat. Thus the retreat actually began a week before the enemy made contact on 8 April. It was considered that the new position – on the Aliakmon – could be held only if the Greek contingents were able to stand firm and if the Yugoslav forces in south western Yugoslavia could prevent the Germans from turning the position. Wilson, whose eyes had been opened to the uselessness of the Yugoslav army on 3 April was satisfied that neither of these things would happen. The Greeks were suffering from defeatism, and when they began to withdraw from their forward positions they would not stop before they reached Athens. This would leave the British flank hopelessly exposed. Once again, before the new defensive line had been established, the Commander-in-Chief was planning to withdraw from it – to the Thermopylae line. The decision was taken on 13 April, and four days later – when the retreat to the Thermopylae line was still in progress – representatives of the Joint Planning Staff in Cairo came to Athens to plan on the spot for the evacuation of the whole force from Greece. They had already been studying the subject, however, so that the question of evacuation had been in the mind of the Commander-in-Chief, Middle East, almost from the first exchange of shots with the Germans. So much for *Lustre's* 'reasonable chance of success'.

Mussolini had made it inevitable that Hitler should occupy the mainland of Greece; and belatedly the Führer decided to throw in Crete for good measure. Had the British not committed about 60,000 troops in Greece, Wavell would have had much greater resources to spare for the defence of Crete – which was strategically important to a degree which Greece was not. Instead of being preoccupied with the rescue of as many men as possible from Greece, Middle East Command could have used the available shipping to send fresh troops properly equipped to garrison the Island, rather than to land part of the remnant of *Lustre* there, many of them with nothing to oppose the Germans with but their bare hands.

Had *Lustre* been cancelled at the beginning of March, as it should have been, the Germans would have found Crete an impossibly tough proposition.

That is, if the inertia and incompetence of the first five months of British occupation had been replaced with dynamic preparation in the last month before the Germans arrived. This is a moot point. The real fault lay with the higher command, and perhaps it could not be expected to change its outlook overnight. This view is supported by Wavell's reaction to the highly-critical report of the Inter-Services Committee on the loss of Crete. He was given a copy as soon as it was written, but did not even trouble to read it. This seems extraordinary. It was his duty to read such a report so that the lessons it contained – and there were many – could be applied in future operations. To ignore it was the absolute negation of one of his most important functions as Commander-in-Chief. Apart from this it might be thought that mild curiosity as to what his professional colleagues had made of the disaster of Crete would have tempted him to glance inside the document.

It was only when he had assumed command in India, and had become aware that the report was being widely studied by those who did not want to make the same mistakes again that he himself read it. Predictably, he rejected many of its findings. The Inter-Services Committee was supposed to be looking at the facts, and not criticizing the operation 'from the higher point of view'. They had examined Crete in isolation, and had paid no attention to the difficulties he faced in other parts of his command. They had taken no evidence from the commanders. In the particular circumstances of the Middle East it had been impossible to undertake a large programme of defence works in Crete – Royal Engineers personnel, stores, material, transport, labour, all were utterly insufficient. All the able-bodied men had left the Island.[5] (The report had suggested that there were still in Crete 400,000 people, anxious to defend their homes. Many of them

[5] AIR 8/545.

would have been delighted to wield a pick and shovel for this purpose – had there been any picks and shovels for them to use.)

The Prime Minister was no less critical than the Inter-Services Committee. He wrote on 14 June in a minute aimed at the Chiefs of Staff Committee:

> I cannot feel that there was any real grip shown by Middle East H.Q. upon this operation of the defence of Crete. They regarded it as a tiresome commitment while at the same time acquiescing in its strategic importance. No-one in high authority seems to have sat down for two or three mornings together and endeavoured to take a full forward view of what would happen in the light of our information, so fully given, and the many telegrams sent by me and the Chiefs of Staff about *Scorcher*. No-one seems to have said 'We have got to hold the place with practically no air support. What then should be our policy about airfields and the counter-attacks of paratroops or other airborne landings. What supplies and equipment are necessary, and how do we get them in?' The food difficulty was not mentioned to us. The non-removal of the *bouches inutiles* was a great fault, although some I believe were taken off. It is true that some of the supplies were sunk en route. The slowness in acting on the precise intelligence with which they were furnished, and the general evidence of lack of drive and precision filled me with disquiet about this Middle East Staff. It is evident that very far-reaching steps will have to be taken.[6]

The Germans were of course highly satisfied with the success of *Marita*, and in spite of its very heavy cost they made the most of *Merkur*. The capture of Crete was seen to have many strategic benefits. It was a great blow to British prestige in the Middle East, and could lead to unrest among the Arabs which might make its effect felt as far afield as India. Churchill's personal position was endangered, and the United States would now think twice about helping the allies. Any doubt about Turkey's neutrality must be removed, and the French government

[6] PREM 3/109, ff. 32-3.

would be more likely to work in close collaboration with the Reich. Italian morale, sadly in need of a boost, would be improved.[7]

The navy were quick to capitalize on the capture of Crete, for it seemed that there might now be a chance of realizing Raeder's dream of using the eastern Mediterranean as a springboard to defeat the British in the Middle East. Indeed, on 24 May when the fate of Crete still hung in the balance, it was pointed out that possession of the Island would have immense significance for German strategy in the area.[8]

This theme was developed in a strategic survey of the eastern Mediterranean dated 1 June, in which the navy was quite carried away by the possibilities. The occupation of the whole Adriatic coast, the Greek Islands in the Aegean, and Crete had opened up undreamed of opportunities. Offensive operations by sea and air would now be possible against Britain's bases in the eastern Mediterranean. The stage was set for the decisive battle against her, since the most sensitive points in the Empire now lay at the mercy of the Reich. She was in mortal danger, and knew it. The main German and Italian aim must be to destroy the British Mediterranean fleet, and although *Barbarossa* was now in the forefront of the Wehrmacht's mind that fact must not be allowed to lessen or delay the offensive in the Mediterranean. As the Italians could not be counted on for the necessary drive and determination future operations would have to be under German leadership, or at least there must be greater influence on the Italians than hitherto.

The whole brilliant war-winning campaign was then sketched out. France must be made to assure the position in Syria so that the danger of a British attack would be ruled out, and she must be armed to help in a future German operation against British power in the Middle East. The Luftwaffe would bomb the Suez Canal and the Red Sea from Syria. Tobruk should be captured as soon

[7] MOD 51/94.
[8] *Ibid.* 50/77-80.

as possible. Malta would be next in line, and then Gibraltar, leaving Alexandria and Suez as the final goals. The navy was so convinced that domination of the eastern Mediterranean and the elimination of all British military power and political influence from the area were fundamental to the whole German strategy that in spite of other important calls on the Wehrmacht, including *Barbarossa*, operations on the lines they had suggested should proceed at all costs – before United States help could reach Britain in significant quantities.[9] Raeder had said all this before, and although the case was now ten times stronger with the capture of Crete Hitler was too deeply immersed in Russia to spare any thought for the navy's plans, which, as has been said above, could have won the war for him.

Perhaps the last word should be with the Australians who, like the New Zealanders, took a great deal on trust when they agreed that their volunteer citizen armies should go to Greece, and did not insist that they should be evacuated from Crete before they were committed irrevocably to the hopeless defence of the Island. In November 1941 the Australian government – which had been in opposition at the time of the Greece and Crete campaigns – were consulted by Britain about the possibility of using their troops in Turkey. They were much more cautious than their predecessors had been in the spring. They pointed out that the information which had then been supplied about the proposed campaigns had reached them only in sketchy outline through the Advisory War Council on which they were represented; and now that they were in office they were very disturbed to find out for the first time (through the Commander-in-Chief of the Australian Forces) about the shortcomings in implementing the plan for the Greek campaign. For example, compared with the agreed order of battle of 126,000 men, only two-fifths of that number had gone to Greece; only eight air squadrons had operated there, as against the twenty-three planned

[9] MOD 51/82-91.

for; the troops sent had been relatively untrained; and so on. Therefore before they could agree that their troops should now go to Turkey they would need firm assurances about the chance of success. In fact, once bitten, twice shy.

A telegram was drafted to attempt to answer these points. The draft said that the present Australian government's information about the Greek campaign was obviously incomplete. For example, although it was admitted that the strength of the force actually sent was less than had been planned, it was because of the critical situation that had arisen in the Western Desert. The British government had no knowledge of a decision to send twenty-three squadrons – the correct figure was twenty, which would have been built up by the middle of the year.

When the CIGS saw the draft he suggested that it should be strengthened by pointing out that although the allies might have suffered a tactical defeat in Greece the strategic gains had been immense, and might well prove to be decisive in the long run. The German offensive against Russia had been delayed, and no one could say what this might cost them. Further, the allied expedition had unquestionably led to the *coup d'état* in Yugoslavia, and the determination of that country to resist the Germans. She had been transformed from being a passive onlooker into an effective ally, within whose borders resistance still burned, ready to flame up again as soon as the day of reckoning drew near.

In the end Churchill decided, wisely, not to answer Curtin, the new Australian Prime Minister, point by point. Although it was possible to try to defend the decision to send an expeditionary force to Greece by using pious-hope arguments of the sort adduced by Dill, it was also possible to demonstrate that *Lustre* had led directly to a serious weakening of the British strategic position in the Mediterranean, that it had removed from the fight against Hitler thirty thousand British, Australian and New Zealand servicemen, three cruisers, six destroyers, and well over 300,000 tons of merchant shipping; and that all this appalling loss could have been avoided had the War Cabinet been able to understand, not the distant future but simply the immediate present when they took their decision – that the balance of power in the Balkans had changed so much in Germany's favour that it was no longer safe to go there, that the allied position in North Africa was not secure, that the Yugoslav army was a broken reed, that *Lustre* could do little more than scamper into Greece and scamper out again, and above all that it was Crete, not Greece, that really mattered.

It was certainly better to let sleeping dogs lie. To the Australian Prime Minister Churchill merely said: 'I do not think that you will wish me at the moment to reply in full to the detailed points made regarding the Greece and Crete campaigns, although clearly there is much that might be said . . .'[10]

With this summing-up there can hardly be serious disagreement.

[10] PREM 3/206/2, f. 11.

BIBLIOGRAPHY

Books and published works

ANSEL, Walter: *Hitler and the Middle Sea*, Durham, N.C., 1972.

AVON, The Earl of: *The Eden Memoirs: The Reckoning*, London, Cassell, 1965.

BUCKLEY, Christopher: *Greece and Crete, 1941*, London, HMSO, 1952.

BUTLER, J. R. M.: *Grand Strategy*, II, London, HMSO, 1957.

CERVI, Mario: *The Hollow Legions: Mussolini's Blunder in Greece, 1940-41*, London, Chatto and Windus, 1972.

CHURCHILL, Winston S.: *The Second World War* (6 volumes), London, Cassell, 1948-54.

CIANO, Galeazzo: *Diary, 1939-43* (Ed. Malcolm Muggeridge), London, Heinemann, 1947.

CUNNINGHAM OF HYNDHOPE, Admiral of the Fleet Viscount: 'The Battle of Crete', *London Gazette Supplement*, 1948.

————: 'Transportation of the army to Greece and the evacuation of the army from Greece, 1941', *London Gazette Supplement*, 1948.

————: *A Sailor's Odyssey*, London, Hutchinson, 1951.

D'ALBIAC, Air Marshal Sir J. H.: 'Air Operations in Greece, 1940-41', *London Gazette Supplement*, 1947.

DAVIN, D. M.: *Crete (Official History of New Zealand in the Second World War)*, Wellington, Department of Internal Affairs, 1953; London, Oxford University Press, 1953.

DE GUINGAND, Major-General Sir Francis W.: *Operation Victory*, London, Hodder and Stoughton, 1947.

HALDER, Generaloberst Franz: *Kriegstagebuch*, II, Stuttgart, W. Kohlhammer Verlag, 1963.

KIPPENBERGER, Major-General Sir H.: *Infantry Brigadier*, London, Oxford University Press, 1949.

LONG, Gavin: *Greece, Crete and Syria*, Canberra, Australian War Memorial, 1953.

MCCLYMONT, W. G.: *To Greece (Official History of New Zealand in the Second World War)*, Wellington, Department of Internal Affairs, 1959.

MACKENZIE, Sir Compton: *Wind of Freedom: The history of*

the invasion of Greece by the Axis powers *1940-41*,
London, Chatto and Windus, 1943.

PAPAGOS, General Alexandros: *The Battle of Greece,
1940-41* (Tr. Pat. Eliascos), Athens, Scazikis, 1949.

PLAYFAIR, I. S. O.: *The Mediterranean and the Middle East*,
I and II, London, HMSO, 1954, 1956.

STEWART, I. McD. G.: *The Struggle for Crete*, London,
Oxford University Press, 1966.

THOMAS, D. A.: *Crete: The battle at sea*, London, Deutsch,
1972.

TOYNBEE, A. and V. (Eds.): *Survey of International Affairs:
The Initial Triumph of the Axis*, London, Oxford University Press, 1958.

TREVOR-ROPER, H. R.: *Hitler's War Directives*, London,
Sidgwick and Jackson, 1964.

*VAN CREVELD, Martin L.: *Hitler's Strategy, 1940-41: The
Balkan Clue*, London, Cambridge University Press, 1973.

WAVELL OF CYRENAICA AND WINCHESTER, Field-Marshal
Lord: 'Operations in the Middle East from 7th February,
1941 to 15th July, 1941', *London Gazette Supplement*,
1946.

WOODWARD, Sir E. Llewellyn: *British Foreign Policy in the
Second World War* (5 volumes), London, HMSO, 1970-
in progress.

Documents and official sources

Documents on German Foreign Policy, Series D (1937-41),
London, HMSO, 1954-62.
The Greek White Book, London, 1942.

Chief of Air Staff Papers (Public Record Office)
AIR 8/545   Crete: operations. April-October
1941.

* AUTHOR'S NOTE: At the time of going to press I had not yet seen
Martin L. van Creveld's article 'Prelude to Disaster: The British
Decision to Aid Greece, 1940-41', *Journal of Contemporary History*,
ix, 1974.

Cabinet Papers (PRO)
CAB 65   War Cabinet Minutes.
CAB 66   War Cabinet Memoranda.
CAB 69   Defence Committee: operations.

Foreign Office Papers (PRO)
FO 371/24892   Eastern front: Balkan situation. 1940.
FO 371/24916   Aircraft and war material for Greece. 1940.
FO 371/29722-4   Bulgarian-German relations and Bulgaria's accession to the Tripartite Pact. 1941.
FO 371/30205   Yugoslavia and the war. 1941.
FO 371/30243   Anglo-Yugoslav relations. 1941.

Ministry of Defence – Naval Historical Branch (microfilms)
MOD 50   *Kriegstagebuch*, Director of Naval Warfare, Part C XIII.
MOD 51   *Kriegstagebuch*, Director of Naval Warfare, Part C XIV.
MOD 90   Directorate of Naval Warfare. *Marita*.
MOD 91   Directorate of Naval Warfare. *Marita*.
MOD 578   *Deutsches Marinekommando Italien, Akte 'Operative Absichten, 1940-41'*.

Prime Minister's Office Papers (PRO)
PREM 3/109   Crete: November 1940-September 1942.
PREM 3/206/1   Greece: British and Imperial campaign. Australian and New Zealand forces. April 1941.
PREM 3/206/2   Telegrams exchanged with Australia concerning conduct of campaign. November 1941-January 1942.
PREM 3/206/3   Various: February 1941-March 1942.

PREM 3/294/1   Report on Foreign Secretary's visit to Middle East. February-April 1941.

PREM 3/308   Telegrams exchanged with Secretary of State for War. October-November 1940.

PREM 3/309/1   Principal telegrams relating to operations August 1940-February 1941 (printed).

National Archives of the United States (microfilm)

T 78/329
Frames 6285489-655   *Bulgarische Grenzregelung in Jugoslawien.* Material on *Marita* April-May 1941.

T 821/127
Frames 1-440   Italian Supreme Command. Correspondence, memoranda, plans, and other records of the War Ministry concerning the invasion of Greece. June 1940-May 1941.

————
Frames 538-628   Italian Supreme Command. Situation reports on military operations along Greco-Albanian border. October-November 1940.

T 821/129
Frames 96-274   Italian Supreme Command. Correspondence concerning the transfer of units to Albania. November 1940-April 1941.

————
Frames 461-689   Italian Supreme Command. Miscellaneous records of the campaign against Greece. November 1940-May 1941.

T 821/207
Frames 282-591   Directives issued by Generals Soddu and Cavallero. November 1940-April 1941.

Military Headquarters Papers – Middle East Forces (PRO)

WO 201/11   Greece: operations. November 1940-February 1941.

WO 201/45   Greece: HQ British troops 'out' signals. March-April 1941.

WO 201/52   Conversation between General Wilson and General Papagos. March-April 1941.

WO 201/54	Greek campaign: Inter-Services report. March-April 1941.
WO 201/55	Middle East to Greece and Crete reinforcement policy. October-November 1940.
WO 201/56	Middle East to Greece and Crete reinforcement policy. November-December 1940.
WO 201/57	Middle East to Greece and Crete reinforcement policy. December 1940-May 1941.
WO 201/72	Report on military operations. 19 May 1941.
WO 201/98	British Military Mission to Greece: staff duties matters. October 1940-June 1941.
WO 201/99	Crete: Inter-Services report on operations. November 1940-June 1941.
WO 201/100	Greece: British Liaison Staff operations. January-June 1941.
WO 201/2652	Greece and Crete: extracts from report by an Inter-Services Committee on operations. November 1940-April 1941.
WO 201/2727	Force Barbarity: planning November 1940.

INDEX

Index

Index

Index

Index

205

Index